Robert Peterson lays the _____ e only solid ground for assurance of salvation and _____ on that foundation with the doctrines of the Holy Spirit's comforting testimony and holy fruit. This book radiates scriptural clarity and heartfelt compassion for people struggling to find rest for their souls in God's everlasting love.

JOEL R. BEEKE, president, Puritan
Reformed Theological Seminary

This treatment of assurance weaves together a rare combination of biblical study and practical outworking. The former includes the assurance built into the promises of the gospel, the confirming work of the Spirit, and the attesting witness of a transformed life; the latter deploys many stories and years of pastoral experience. This book promises to bring godly confidence and quiet comfort to many troubled believers.

D. A. CARSON, professor emeritus of New
Testament, Trinity Evangelical Divinity School

In this well-crafted book on assurance, Robert Peterson brings to bear a wealth of experience in teaching, writing, and ministering to make one of his best contributions to the church. Not only does this volume reflect a lifetime of thought on the doctrine of perseverance, it also flows from a pastor's heart, as well as from the author's deep experience of walking with the Lord. The work is filled with careful biblical exegesis, wise theological insight, and real-life anecdotes. There are other fine books on the believer's assurance of salvation, but this one sets a new standard.

DANIEL EBERT, president, Christian
Training and Missionary Fellowship

Sooner or later, every Christian wonders, "Am I *really* a Christian? Jesus might be real. But am I?" This bewildering, terrifying, common experience is why Robert Peterson has written *The Assurance of Salvation: Biblical Hope for Our Struggles.* This honest and biblical book guides us away from saying to God, "But this time I really mean it," and toward hearing God say to us, "I will never leave you nor forsake you."

RAY ORTLUND, pastor, Immanuel Church, Nashville

This useful and enlightening study combines personal testimonies, biblical exposition, and pastoral counsel. The result is a highly readable survey of the all-important theme of Christian assurance. Writing with admirable brevity and clarity, the author covers dozens of the most important biblical passages in an organized and creative fashion. Most Christians struggle with assurance at some point, sometimes at multiple points. This book connects readers with resources to diagnose their spiritual insecurity and restore their confidence in Christ. It is well suited for both personal and small group use.

ROBERT W. YARBROUGH, professor of New Testament, Covenant Theological Seminary

THE
ASSURANCE
OF
SALVATION

BIBLICAL HOPE FOR
OUR STRUGGLES

ROBERT A. PETERSON

ZONDERVAN

The Assurance of Salvation
Copyright © 2019 by Robert A. Peterson

ISBN 978-0-310-51632-3 (softcover)

ISBN 978-0-310-10717-0 (audio)

ISBN 978-0-310-51633-0 (ebook)

Requests for information should be addressed to:
Zondervan, *3900 Sparks Dr. SE, Grand Rapids, Michigan 49546*

Cover design: Bruce Gore | Gore Studio, Inc.
Cover image: Pexels.com
Interior design: Kait Lamphere

Printed in the United States of America

19 20 21 22 23 24 25 26 /LSC/ 15 14 13 12 11 10 9 8 7 6 5 4 3 2 1

CONTENTS

INTRODUCTION

The true stories that follow may differ in their details, but they share one thing in common.

- A godly Christian woman who lacked assurance sought help at the lecture of a famous evangelical writer. He told her that he didn't talk to people at his lectures. When she explained how far she had travelled to see him, he conceded: "Okay, you have five minutes." Needless to say, she received little help from him and was disillusioned by the experience.
- Jim could not defeat his persistent jealousy of his neighbors, and his confidence in salvation was tied to his success in dealing with his covetous thoughts. As a result, his assurance went up and down like a yoyo in sync with his successes and failures.[1]
- Sally and her husband, Mark, both young college students, came to see me in my office. She described her struggles with assurance. After listening to her story and her clear explanation of the gospel, I asked Mark what he thought. He confessed, "I am more confident about Sally's Christian faith than my own."
- A pastor built his Christian life on perfectly keeping the law. As a result, he lacked the confidence of salvation. A ten-year-old girl in his Sunday school class knew the Lord

with a joyful simplicity. Without realizing it, she was a constant rebuke to the pastor, for he saw in her the assurance he desired.

What is the one thing these stories have in common? Each story shows believers wrestling with assurance. Assurance is confidence in one's final salvation. Almost every believer struggles with the assurance of salvation at some point in his or her Christian experience. You may be struggling with it now, or perhaps you know a loved one or friend who is plagued by doubt. If so, then this book is written for you.

DIFFERENT CONCLUSIONS CONCERNING ASSURANCE

One reason people struggle is that well-meaning Christians reach very different conclusions about assurance. Jon Tal Murphree, a conservative Methodist professor and author, teaches:

> Calvinism holds "once in grace, always in grace," while Arminianism subscribes to "forfeitable grace"—which means the possibility of eventual lostness after having been in a saved condition at an earlier time in life.
>
> Arminianism does not hold that people lose salvation by single acts of sin in moments of weakness, but that they *can* lose salvation by persisting in an unrepentant lifestyle of sin and rebellion against God.
>
> Almost every page of the Bible stands on the underlying assumption that God has placed in human hands an awesome obligation to cooperate with God in defining one's own destiny. Failure to do so even for the Christian believer can be disastrous.[2]

Murphree is an evangelical Christian who loves and serves the Lord. I regard him as a brother in Christ and worthy of respect.

Murphree holds to present assurance of final salvation, as long as one continues in faith. But for Murphree, assurance—and even salvation itself—can be lost. People who were saved by grace may forfeit grace if they persist in a rebellious lifestyle without repentance. Murphree holds that if believers fail to cooperate with God in defining their destiny, they are heading for spiritual disaster.

The well-known *Catechism of the Catholic Church* contains many truths with which all believers can agree: God is the Holy Trinity, the Holy Scriptures are the Word of God, the death and resurrection of Christ are the basis of salvation, and God expects his people to live grateful and holy lives. I am grateful for Roman Catholicism's affirmation of these truths.

Yet I could find no section treating assurance in the eight-hundred-plus pages of the *Catechism of the Catholic Church*. I did find some related themes from which readers may draw conclusions concerning assurance. The catechism speaks of the certainty of faith based on the truthfulness of God and his Word, underscores the necessity of believing in the Father and Son for salvation, and rejoices in God's entirely free gift of faith to human beings. But then the catechism plainly affirms that saving faith can be lost, appealing to 1 Timothy 1:18–19 as proof:

> Faith is certain. It is more certain than all human knowledge because it is founded on the very word of God who cannot lie. . . .
>
> Believing in Jesus Christ and in the One who sent him for our salvation is necessary for obtaining that salvation. . . .
>
> Faith is an entirely free gift that God makes to man. We can lose this priceless gift, as St. Paul indicated to Timothy, "Wage the good warfare, holding faith and a good conscience. By rejecting conscience, certain persons have made shipwreck of their faith [1 Tim. 1:18–19]."[3]

Although I agree that faith's certainty is built on Scripture, that we must trust Christ for salvation, and that faith is God's gift,

I disagree that 1 Timothy 1:18–19 teaches that salvation can be lost. In fact, I devote two chapters to show that God saves *and keeps* his people. My interaction with Catholic friends shows that few enjoy a robust assurance of salvation. This is rooted in the Catholic Church's lack of attention to assurance and to its teaching that believers can fall from grace and be lost.

In contrast to the previous two sources, J. I. Packer, author of the famous book *Knowing God*, writes:

> One more thing must be added to show how great is the blessing of adoption—namely, this: that it is a blessing that *abides*. . . . The depressions, randomnesses, and immaturities that mark the children of broken homes are known to us all. But things are not like that in God's family. There you have absolute stability; the parent is entirely wise and good, and the child's position is permanently assured. The very concept of adoption is itself a proof and guarantee of the preservation of the saints, for only bad fathers throw their sons out of the family, even under provocation; and God is not a bad father, but a good one.
>
> Paul sets before us the adequacy of God as our *sovereign protector*, and the decisiveness of His *covenant commitment* to us. . . . The goal of grace . . . is to create a love-relationship between God and us who believe, the kind of relationship for which man was first made, and the bond of fellowship by which God binds Himself to us is His covenant. He imposes it unilaterally, by promise and command. . . . Once established, the covenant abides, for God keeps it in being. . . . What is being proclaimed here is God's undertaking to uphold and protect us when men and things are threatening, to provide for us as long as our earthly pilgrimage lasts, and to lead us finally into the full enjoyment of Himself, however many obstacles may seem at present to stand in the way of our getting there.[4]

Packer is as committed to grace and holiness as Murphree. Packer agrees with the Catholic catechism that God and his Word are utterly truthful, that faith in Christ (and in the Father) is necessary for salvation, and that faith is God's gracious gift to sinners. But Packer departs from both Murphree and the catechism when he insists that salvation is a permanent gift that God will not revoke and that God's children are therefore safe in his care. For Packer, God preserves all he saves by grace through faith, and consequently, those who rest in the word of God's grace can know comfort and assurance.

To properly understand assurance, we must ask the most important question: What does Scripture say about the possibility of believers in Jesus having confidence of their final salvation? Let's examine a passage that begins to answer the question.

1 JOHN 5:9-13

We accept human testimony, but God's testimony is greater because it is the testimony of God, which he has given about his Son. Whoever believes in the Son of God accepts this testimony. Whoever does not believe God has made him out to be a liar, because they have not believed the testimony God has given about his Son. And this is the testimony: God has given us eternal life, and this life is in his Son. Whoever has the Son has life; whoever does not have the Son of God does not have life. I write these things to you who believe in the name of the Son of God so that you may know that you have eternal life.

John first reminds us that we regularly believe what other people tell us. If we have adequate knowledge of someone's character, our default mode is to believe what that person says. If we tend to believe other people, how much more should we believe the words that come from God's holy mouth! God has said many things in his Word and has spoken supremely through his Son,

Jesus Christ (v. 9). Those who trust God's Word know within themselves that he speaks truth (because of the Holy Spirit's inner witness). Doubting God's Word about Christ is equivalent to calling God a liar, a foolish thing to do (v. 10).

Next John describes what God says about his Son: "This is the testimony: God has given us eternal life, and this life is in his Son" (v. 11). God's message about his Son is all about eternal life. God says that eternal life is found in one place—in the Son himself. "The Father has sent his Son to be the Savior of the world" (1 John 4:14). He died and arose to rescue sinners, and all who put their trust in him for salvation receive eternal life.

John divides humanity into the "haves" and the "have-nots." In God's estimation the two groups are not divided by beauty, physical prowess, wealth, or fame, things we so often admire. The haves are distinguished from have-nots by one thing—whether they *have* the Son of God as Savior: "Whoever *has* the Son has life; whoever does not *have* the Son of God does not have life" (5:12, emphasis added). Christ is the difference between heaven and hell, between knowing God and not knowing him, between having and lacking eternal life. The Son of God is the most important person in the world. And knowing him is the most important thing in the world.

John's Purpose Statement

Within this framework stands the purpose statement for 1 John: "I write these things to you who believe in the name of the Son of God so that you may know that you have eternal life" (5:13). Certain passages in 1 John often have been understood as "tests of faith." These passages teach how crucial it is for believers to continue to believe in Christ, live for God, and love one another. I do not deny that these passages can be used as tests of salvation in the hands of a godly pastor or friend to help someone walking away from the Lord. But 1 John's historical context suggests that "evidence of faith" is a more accurate description of these passages than "tests of faith."

The historical situation of 1 John sheds light on the letter. John is not writing to backsliding Christians whose lives had brought their professions of faith into question. He is writing to battered and bruised Christians.[5] False teachers tried to convince them of faulty things about Jesus (4:1–6) and the Christian life (1:8–10). When the false teachers were unable to win their case, they rejected John's readers and departed (2:18–19). John says, in effect, "Good riddance!" The false teachers left because they did not belong to Jesus. John praises his readers for not following the false teachings and for continuing in the truth that they heard from him. He writes to comfort them after their rejection by the false teachers. He wants them to look at God's work in their lives and gain confidence that they have eternal life. John's readers strengthen their assurance of salvation by walking in faith, love, and holiness. John does not want to condemn but to encourage. He writes to strengthen believers' assurance. Contrary to what some say, God wants those who trust Christ for salvation to have confidence that they belong to him. He wants them to "know" that they have eternal life.

Evidence of Eternal Life

How do they know? This is where the evidence of eternal life comes in. God ministers assurance of salvation to us by the promises of his Word, by the inner working of his Spirit, and by changing our lives. Here in 1 John, the apostle emphasizes the third way God assures us. John wants his readers to be assured by the fact that their lives exhibit faith, love, and holiness. They believe the right things about Jesus (5:1). They love one another (3:14). The basic tenor of their lives is holiness, not sin (5:18–19). Their changed and changing lives are evidence of eternal life.

ROADMAP

Where will our journey to assurance take us? As Packer indicates, Scripture offers abundant assurance to believers in Christ.

However, various difficulties hinder our enjoyment of "the full assurance that faith brings" (Heb. 10:22). Chapter 1 examines the people and things that trouble assurance.

As we saw, God assures us in three main ways: by promising salvation in his Word, by the Holy Spirit's ministering in our hearts, and by God's working in our lives. Chapters 2 through 4 focus on the first of these. Chapter 2 argues that the gospel itself brings assurance. Chapters 3 and 4 show that the apostles John (in his gospel and first epistle) and Paul (in his letters), respectively, wrote to fortify Christians with confidence of final salvation.

Chapter 5 deals with the identity and works of the Holy Spirit, and chapter 6 explores how the Spirit assures our hearts of God's love and salvation. Chapter 7 examines the roles that changed lives play in assurance. Chapter 8 introduces God's antidote to the troublers—defenders of assurance. It sets them in the biblical context for assurance—the church. The defenders are the ministries of God's Word, Spirit, and people that God uses to help others and to strengthen those who minister. The conclusion encourages strugglers (all of us at times!) to receive as full a measure of assurance as we can from our gracious God.

CHAPTER 1

"TROUBLERS" OF ASSURANCE

The troublers are the problem. There are many troublemakers in the Bible, but only two are called "troublers." And even one of those troublers was falsely accused—the man who accused him was the real troubler! In Scripture a troubler is one who disobeys the clear command of the Lord to the detriment of the people of God.[1]

The first troubler is "Achan, the troubler of Israel, who broke faith in the matter of the devoted thing" (1 Chron. 2:7 ESV). Achan's sin led to Israel's defeat at Ai in the promised land, when an Israelite army fled before a smaller army because "the hearts of the people melted in fear and became like water" (Josh. 7:5). When Joshua fell on his face before the Lord and asked the reason for this defeat, the Lord explained. He said that Israel had broken covenant with him by stealing and lying. The Lord had commanded his people, when they were victorious at Jericho, to engage in religious purification by devoting the city and everything in it to the Lord for destruction. Achan had disobeyed the Lord's explicit instruction by taking a beautiful robe, silver, and gold (vv. 20–21). Because Achan took things the Lord had devoted to destruction, Israel itself became "devoted to destruction" (v. 12). That is why they experienced defeat at Ai. Achan truly was a troubler of Israel.

The second troubler, however, only actually troubled the Lord's enemies. God raised up the prophet Elijah to confront the wicked king Ahab. How wicked was Ahab?

> Ahab son of Omri did more evil in the eyes of the LORD than any of those before him. . . . He also married Jezebel daughter of Ethbaal king of the Sidonians, and began to serve Baal and worship him. . . . Ahab . . . did more to arouse the anger of the LORD, the God of Israel, than did all the kings of Israel before him. (1 Kings 16:30–31, 33)

Ahab was exceedingly wicked. For that reason, he hated Elijah, who had the courage to rebuke him for his idolatry. As a judgment, Elijah had prophesied that there would be no rain in Israel except at his word. This divinely ordained drought went on for three years and led to the dramatic contest on Mount Carmel between Elijah and 450 prophets of Baal and 400 prophets of Asherah. After the false prophets failed miserably to call down fire upon their offering to Baal, Yahweh showed that he is the true and living God by sending fire from heaven to consume a burnt offering, wood, stones, dust, and water in the trench around the sacrifice (18:36–39). As a result, the false prophets were put to the sword, and God sent rain by Elijah's word (vv. 40, 45).

Before this contest Elijah sent for Ahab. When the evil king saw God's prophet, the king said, "Is that you, you troubler of Israel?" (v. 17). Elijah, not one to back down from a confrontation, threw the accusation back at Ahab, "I have not made trouble for Israel. . . . But you and your father's family have. You have abandoned the LORD's commands and have followed the Baals" (v. 18). Elijah then challenged Ahab to gather the false prophets to Mount Carmel for the contest mentioned above.

Achan was a troubler of Israel, and contrary to Ahab's charge, Ahab was the troubler, not Elijah. Yet troublers not only appear in Scripture but also in our lives. Unfortunately, every believer in Christ has troublers too. Such troublers can come in many forms.

An important type are those problems or people that hinder believers' assurance of salvation. This book is about those troublers. Christians agree that assurance of salvation is a wonderful thing. They disagree on some of the details, as I explained in the introduction. But all agree that assurance is healthy and desirable. The troublers of assurance are the problem.

Before seeing from Scripture how God grants assurance of salvation, we need to get to know some of these troublers. Three words of caution are in order. First, categories of troublers of assurance could easily be multiplied. Below are key categories that are representative of other ones. Second, the categories are not watertight compartments. The problems most people have when struggling with assurance do not fit neatly into one category. But often one category predominates. Third, I plan to return to the troublers in subsequent chapters when discussing the ways God graciously assures his children that they belong to him. Let's listen to stories for each of the five categories of troublers of assurance:

1. Difficult backgrounds
2. Intellectual doubts
3. Sensitive hearts, strong emotions, and fear
4. Hypocrisy and apostasy
5. Overconfidence

TROUBLER 1: DIFFICULT BACKGROUNDS

A difficult background can be a major troubler. Some have trouble putting their background behind them and moving forward. I'll also consider the related issue of those who have a propensity to doubt because of a difficult background.

An Absent and Cold Father

For years Erica did not believe that God loved and accepted her. The roots of her troubles ran deep. Her mother and father separated and then divorced when she was nine. However, it was not a clean break. From time to time her father would come back, but he always left again. Erica described standing in the driveway watching her father drive away and feeling rejected. Each time it happened, her sense of rejection only intensified. Her father was cold and distant and failed to communicate love. Erica was a Christian when she entered college and still wanted her father's approval and love. She loved God but never felt completely accepted by him. Her sense of God's approval ebbed and flowed according to how well she performed a certain set of Christian duties. These problems continued for years.

A Propensity to Doubt

In Ruth Tucker's candid and helpful book *Walking Away from Faith: Unraveling the Mystery of Belief and Unbelief,* Tucker, an experienced professor of missiology and church history, bares her soul.[2] She deals with losing faith, considers historical and contemporary challenges to Christianity, and includes stories of people who walked away from the faith along with stories of those who returned.

Most helpful to me is her candid report of her ongoing struggle with unbelief as a Christian leader. Even while she continues with God in worship, fellowship, and service, she struggles, sometimes mightily, with unbelief. Why? Her conclusion bears repeating, "I accept the conflicts and questions as part of my psychological and spiritual makeup, which allows me to humbly reach out to those with similar struggles."[3] She surely does help others as her book attests.

Does she give us any clues as to how she came to have such a "psychological and spiritual makeup"? The answer is yes. Her own religious background allowed for little blending of head and heart. She tells how the country church of her childhood introduced her to a heart religion that included altar calls and revivals. Others in the church claimed to have received miracles, visions, and heard voices, but she did not and felt left out. She explains, "I reached out to God the only way I knew how—through my emotions, my heart."[4]

Ruth's young adult years were spent in a fundamentalist setting, where rational biblical literalism replaced experience. Head triumphed over heart. But this too brought her no closer to God. Even now, she explains, "My *secular* life became more and more separated from my *spiritual* life. This dualism of *reason* and *heart* continues for me today."[5] She thus traces for us her background and experiences that have contributed and still contribute to her lack of assurance.

Does she despair as she struggles, sometimes on the border between faith and doubt? Does she forsake the Christian faith? The answer to both questions is a loud no. As she explains,

> Unlike these who have abandoned the faith, I will not—if for no other reason than the mysterious fact that God has a grip on me. Besides, this is my culture, my tradition. I love the Bible stories and the old hymns of the faith. . . . This is my faith, and I will never abandon it—nor will God abandon me.
>
> But do I believe it? If everything depended on my belief, there are some days when, I think, I would be doomed. But my salvation does not depend on the strength of my faith; it depends only on God's grace. Even when my faith is weak, I have confidence in God's hold on my life.[6]

I wish everyone Tucker mentions in her book persevered in the face of challenges as she does. But, sadly, this is not the case. For some, the troublers of assurance are so overwhelming that they give up the fight; they drop out of the race. My prayer is that this book will help some of them. And perhaps believers will find in it some things they can use to help their wavering friends.

TROUBLER 2: INTELLECTUAL DOUBTS

A huge source of difficulty for many is intellectual problems with the Christian faith and the doubts they spawn. Christine Wicker, a journalist, tells of her leaving the faith in her memoir, *God Knows My Heart*.[7] She grew up in fundamentalist Christianity. She credits college and church with destroying her inherited faith. She became disillusioned by the Bible's portrayal of a good and sovereign God who allows so many innocent people to suffer. When she studied other religions in college and learned of millions who worship other gods and who seem to be as good as Christians she knew, her faith took another hit.[8]

Wicker was not about to let others do her thinking for her, certainly not preachers of the Bible. She explains concerning faith, "I had to accept a narrow, handed-down wisdom from people who told me I was a filthy sinner with a brain that wasn't worth using. Without it, I could explore a huge world filled with new ideas."[9] She candidly explains what she believes in today:

> My own idea of God is, of course, merely one I made up. I started with the idea that God understands my heart, as my mother said, and from there everything fell into question. But once again, I made up my theology, gave up on having anyone else agree, kept quiet about it, and then began to see it reflected in unexpected places. I've already mentioned that Nouwen said God is the one who calls us beloved. That's fairly close to being the one who knows my heart.[10]

In fairness, not everyone who rejects Christianity for intellectual reasons openly creates their own private religion, as Christine has done. And not all intellectual apostates feel a need to "go public" with their doubts. Troublers of faith and assurance take many forms. The next example shows us one such form.

Scientific Doubts

Scot McKnight is frank: "In my research of stories of those who have . . . abandoned the faith, the scientific evidence is the most common collision point."[11] Supposed clashes between science and Christianity have led many to question their faith and some to leave faith behind. Christians have sometimes presented creationism in ways that do harm. At times a climate is created in Christian schools and in Sunday school that discourages students from asking difficult questions. This is wrong and hurts those who seek the honest truth. Instead, questions should be encouraged, and teachers need to learn where to get answers. My purpose here is not to try to solve the problems generated by faith and science. But I point readers to resources that offer guidance.[12]

Sometimes Christians have "defended the faith" by misrepresenting and belittling views they reject. Christine Rosen, who eventually left the Christian faith, remembers how her third-grade teacher in a Christian school spoke about creation and evolution:

> "Genesis," her teacher announced, "tells us everything!"
> Christine comments: "This was odd."
> "'Evolution,' her teacher exclaimed, 'says we all come from apes and monkeys!' . . . as if she were describing pigs flying."
> This, for Christine, was a clinching comment: "You've been to the zoo," she concluded. "Who do you think is right, Darwin or God? When she put it that way, I thought, I guess I'd have to choose God."[13]

Christine never forgot what her teacher said that day, although she learned a lesson her teacher did not intend: Christians have all the answers, and people who ask scientific questions are to be dismissed as ignorant fools. Christine's bad experience lingered and "was in part the catalyst that broke the spine of her orthodox faith."[14]

There is little doubt that Ruth Tucker is correct, "The greatest scientific assault against the Christian faith came from Charles Darwin's theory of evolution in the last decades of the nineteenth century. According to Richard Dawkins, 'Darwin made it possible to be an intellectually fulfilled atheist.'"[15]

Consider another example: An adult convert, Sam, is intelligent, gifted, and likeable. He studied Scripture and theology, was a committed believer, and served as a lay officer in his local church. His study of Darwinian evolution progressed from a fascination to adoption of a total worldview. The findings of science convinced him that Scripture was inaccurate and the Christian faith empty. Evolution left no place for the supernatural. His scientific commitments led him to stop praying and reading the Bible. In Sam's opinion he found the truth, and he remains resolute in his commitment to it. Doubts generated by science became big-time troublers of his faith, including salvation and the assurance that once belonged to it.

TROUBLER 3: SENSITIVE HEARTS, STRONG EMOTIONS, AND FEAR

Sensitivity, emotions, and fear are all gifts from God. He created us as sensitive beings, able to respond to one another. He gave us emotions, which are a source of joy. And as children we learn the proper fear of danger. These three gifts, however, can become troublers in our lives.

Sensitive Hearts and Strong Emotions

"I am by nature and upbringing a person of strong emotions." So wrote a student whom I will call Steve in a paper for a class on assurance that I taught some time ago. He went on to explain that his emotionalism shows itself in two main ways. First, he often has strong emotional reactions to situations and circumstances. He learns intuitively and often *feels* something to be true before he can prove it in other ways. Many times, this is helpful and steers him in the right direction. Second, he admits that when he lacks a strong emotional reaction, he longs for one. This propensity sometimes lands him in trouble.

Steve's longing for an emotional reaction has caused him to wrestle with the assurance of salvation. Undoubtedly, it is a troubler in his life. "There are many days when I do not *feel* God's love toward me," he says. He correctly regards his emotional bent as a blessing and a curse. He hungers for a deep experience of God. He rejoices in worship, reading the Word, and prayer. God uses his sensitive heart to pick up signals of others' needs that many would miss. Steve's compassion has helped many in a ministry of counseling and empathy. But he admits that his yearning for emotional experiences with God does not always lead him into the light:

> Yet there is a darker and more dangerous side to this longing. I require more of God than his Word promises and displays. I look for experiences that will somehow fill up the emotional deficiency in my life. At times I become restless, depressed, and desperate. Too often I ignore the manifold blessings in my life in a bid to find that elusive "something more." I am not proud of this, and having recognized it, I am taking steps to bring my emotionalism under control.

By God's grace Steve has learned and is still learning to cope with the down times. We will consider how this plays out later when we examine the delightful ways that God assures his children of their salvation. By his own admission Steve's emotional nature sometimes leads him into religious ecstasy and other times plunges him into spiritual turmoil. His sensitive heart and strong emotions are major troublers of his peace and assurance. He writes, "What about those days when I feel desperate or abandoned by God? . . . There have been times in my life when all I could do was hold onto the Word and walk in darkness." This is the right thing to do in such dark times.

Fear

Fear can be another crippling troubler. The prophet Elijah has a surprising story of paralyzing fear. He trembled at the threat of Jezebel, the wicked wife of wicked king Ahab. Remarkably, this is a continuation of the story earlier in this chapter. Elijah had been so strong in the Lord. He withstood Ahab, brought a drought on Israel at God's command, called down fire from heaven to defeat the multitude of false prophets at Mount Carmel, slaughtered them, brought rain by praying to God after three years of drought, and ran almost seventeen miles to Jezreel (1 Kings 18). Elijah was at the top of his game. He had won! He had spectacularly defeated the prophets of Baal and Asherah and had literally destroyed them. The heavens had closed and opened at his word. He was the man!

Sometimes things change so quickly. When Ahab told Jezebel of Elijah's triumph over and destruction of the prophets she supported, she was furious. She sent a messenger to Elijah with this menacing promise: "May the gods deal with me, be it ever so severely, if by this time tomorrow I do not make your life like that of one of them" (19:2). How did the prophet of God and formerly fearless champion respond to the evil queen's threat? "Elijah was afraid, and ran for his life" (v. 3). At first blush, this is difficult to understand. Elijah, who had vanquished 850 prophets at Mount Carmel, now fears the threats of one woman? Os Guinness writes:

> Here is Elijah at the high point of his ministry, recognized, vindicated, successful. Everything seems to be his for the taking. The crowds were behind him, the royal power was humbled, his enemies were largely wiped out, his cause was vindicated, and then suddenly at the threat from one woman—Jezebel—his courage crumples, and he runs for his life. Nothing appears more unreasonable.[16]

Seen from another angle, Elijah's fear and flight make good sense, as Guinness explains:

> Elijah has snapped under the strain of the emotional intensity. The grueling demands of public confrontation have summoned up and exhausted his reserves of strength. The lonely years in the desert followed by the dramatic road race to Jezreel have so stretched his emotions that at a single

threat he folds. It is not God who had let him down but his emotions that had overpowered his faith and reason, and plunged him into a trough of despair.[17]

Even great accomplishments do not necessarily make us immune from fear and doubt, as Elijah's next words reveal: "I have had enough, LORD. . . . Take my life; I am no better than my ancestors" (19:4). Many types of fear can be troublers in our lives and harm our assurance that we are the Lord's. Thoughts of suicide like Elijah's are not always the result, but the many faces of fear can harass the people of God.

TROUBLER 4: HYPOCRISY AND APOSTASY

Although thinking about hypocrisy and apostasy can make us uncomfortable, it is important to do so, for they touch many lives. Hypocrisy is when professing Christians' lives belie their faith. Apostasy is rejection of a faith once professed. Both are troublers of assurance and deserve attention.

Hypocrisy

McKnight serves it to us straight: "Christians, both contemporary and in the entire history of the church—a history which includes moments and events that are incredible by modern standards—create obstacles to faith and sometimes lead believers away from the faith."[18] A powerful example of this is the story of William Lobdell, a *Los Angeles Times* reporter. A conversion experience delivered him from a depressed and desperate life. His career took off when he became the religion beat writer for the paper. "In his column, he reported on the inspirational, altruistic, and holy endeavors of people of faith—men and women who opened up their homes to the homeless, fed the hungry and destitute, and worked to make the world a better place through their piety, mercy, and goodwill."[19]

Since Lobdell's wife had been raised a Roman Catholic, he felt the tug of tradition, and prepared himself for an Easter vigil conversion ceremony. At that very time he began to write about the sex scandals in the Catholic Church and was deeply shaken. He tells his own story:

> I couldn't get the victims' stories or the bishops' lies—many of them right there on their own stationery—out of my head. I had been in journalism more than two decades and had dealt with murders, rapes, other violent crimes and trage-dies. But this was different—the children were so innocent, their parents so faithful, the priests so sick and bishops so corrupt. The life-line Father Vincent had tried to give me began to slip from my hands.[20]

The result? Lobdell could not in good conscience join the Roman Catholic Church. And when he focused on Protestant circles, many results were no better. Phil Zuckerman provides details:

> [Lobdell] followed the likes of charismatic faith-healer-millionaire Benny Hinn, who promises endless streams of poor, suffering people that he'll heal their cancer or diabetes or multiple sclerosis if they just give him all their money. The more [Lobdell] began witnessing unethical Christian scams like this within the Evangelical community, the greater his distaste for religion became.[21]

As the stories of hypocritical Christians piled up, Lobdell's faith could not take it any longer. He explains, "My soul . . . had lost faith long ago. My brain, which had been in denial, had finally caught up. . . . I called my wife on a cellphone. I told her I was putting in for a new beat at the paper."[22] Hypocrisy was the troubler that destroyed Lobdell's faith and assurance. Things don't have to turn out this way, but for many people hypocrisy is an opponent they cannot overcome.

Apostasy

Another irksome troubler for many is the apostasy of others whom they respect. Apostasy is defection from a faith once claimed. This is different than the negative example of professing Christians causing others to stumble. This is the rejection of the faith by someone who formerly professed it, even as a leader. Of course, turning one's back on the Christian faith involves loss of assurance. Apostasy seems to set a particularly upsetting example for some. Ruth Tucker tells the story of Dan Barker, an apostate responsible for many walking away from the faith.

Barker began evangelistic preaching at fifteen, graduated from a Christian college, served three different churches, was a Christian evangelist for eight years, toured, preached, was an accomplished pianist, and wrote songs. To this day he receives royalties from songs he wrote while he was a Christian. But he no longer preaches Christ. Quite the opposite.

> Today Barker uses his evangelistic skills, in speaking and writing, to lead people away from the faith. The testimony of Rhonda Jockisch, posted on a website, is typical. She was a college graduate with a good job, and she was in the habit of reading her Bible daily.
>
> "I should have been on top of the world, and yet I was miserable, full of guilt at all my supposed sins. . . . Then I got a computer and started talking with some humanists/atheists. . . . One of them recommended . . . *Losing Faith in Faith* by Dan Barker. And after reading that book, I knew that if Dan Barker was telling the truth, that there was no way Christianity could be true."[23]

Barker himself did not have a sudden deconversion from Christianity but fell away over four or five years. He satisfied his intellectual hunger with liberal writings until he lost faith entirely. After a period of hypocrisy, in which he continued to preach, he denied the supernatural and never preached again. At least he never preached Christ again; instead he preached an anti-Christian message. His new "ministry" proved successful. He deconverted his parents, who were lay evangelists. He also won his younger brother Darrell over to the atheist cause. In Barker's words, "The gradual change in my parents and brother Darrell was tremendously heartening."[24]

As America's foremost evangelist of unbelief, Barker is as zealous combatting the faith he once espoused as he was promoting it. He enthusiastically writes and speaks for atheism, often debating Christians. He speaks at retirement homes and directs his antimissionary message to children as well as adults. One of his books is titled *Just Pretend: A Free-thought Book for Children.* Though he used to write Christian songs, some of his newer titles include "Nothing Fails Like Prayer" and "Friendly Neighborhood Atheist."[25]

Most who reject Christianity do so more quietly than Dan Barker. Most do not seek to hurt others' faith as he does. Still, apostates are troublers for many people, whose faith is upset and assurance damaged if not robbed altogether.

TROUBLER 5: OVERCONFIDENCE

Some are surprised to hear that overconfidence can be a troubler of assurance. But it certainly can, as Jason's story reveals. A pastor spent much time with Jason, who was living with his girlfriend Krista when they began to move in different directions spiritually. Krista was being drawn to God through the warmth of the pastor's preaching and the kindness of the people of his church. Jason did not see any need for church and did not accompany her there. He thought everything was fine between him and God. He had made a profession of faith in Christ at a youth conference years before. After hearing an evangelist's message about heaven and hell, Jason became scared and at the altar call walked down the aisle.

The pastor tells what happened next and its effect in Jason's life:

When he reached the front of the auditorium, with tears streaming down his face, the speaker asked everyone who had come forward to "repeat this prayer after me." Jason repeated the prayer word for word. When it was over, the speaker declared, "If you just prayed that prayer, you are now a child of God. Heaven is your true home, and you never need to fear hell again. Welcome to the family of God!"

That assurance put Jason at ease. From that moment forward, he rarely thought about heaven or hell again. He hung on to that speaker's promise, believing he was eternally secure in the family of God.[26]

But there was no change in Jason's evil lifestyle. Banking on the assurance the speaker gave him, he sinned without giving it another thought. He regarded those words of assurance as "fire insurance" for hell that allowed him to live as he pleased without giving God a second thought. When Jason and the pastor talked, it became obvious to the pastor that although Jason had some factual knowledge about God, he did not know God personally. He did not have a living relationship with Christ. Despite what the youth-conference speaker told Jason, he was spiritually dead, without hope, and without God in the world (Eph. 2:1, 12).

The careless words of an evangelist misled Jason into overconfidence and a false assurance of salvation. Ironically, a meeting designed to bring people to God became an anesthetic that numbed Jason from feeling a need for a Savior who forgives sins and produces holy lives in those who know and love him. So overconfidence can be counted among the troublers of assurance because it sometimes breeds false assurance. It sings lullabies that put people to sleep, people who need to be awakened to their sin and their need for Jesus. This troubler is difficult to overcome, but more than once, I have seen it happen through God's love.

CONCLUSION

Christians affirm that assurance, confidence of salvation, is beneficial and desirable. But assurance has many enemies. These foes do not announce their presence—"I am a troubler of your salvation and am bent on robbing you of assurance"—but instead wear many disguises.

Sometimes these troublers take the form of a background that makes it difficult to accept God's unconditional love in Christ. At other times they appear as trying experiences that hinder our ability to trust others, including God. Whether through nature or nurture, some of us seem to have a predisposition to doubt God. For such people assurance will always involve fighting a battle, a battle from which some shrink.

Troublers of assurance sometimes morph into intellectual ideas that challenge faith and denigrate it. These troublers make us feel cheated because we believed "such naïve ideas." Feeling enlightened by Darwinism or other philosophies, our worldview shifts until there is no longer a place for God and assurance.

Troublers just won't play fair! They hit us at our weak points, even when we are not looking. Some people are blessed with sensitive hearts that make them aware of others' needs and move them to show compassion. These same sensitive hearts, however, open us up to hurt. Experiences that others cope with prove difficult for us and can lead to questioning our relationship to God.

Some enjoy strong emotions expressed as joy and exhilaration. But these same strong emotions can also produce excessive worry and unhappiness. While some seem untouched by fear, others' lives can be controlled by it if they are not careful. Though they don't announce their role as troublers, sensitive hearts, strong emotions, and fear can upset our emotional and spiritual equilibrium and make us doubt our salvation.

Hypocrisy and apostasy also creep up on many and damage their relationship with God. Many have turned away from the gospel because of the ungodly lives of some who profess to know the Lord. Some intellectual apostates, who scoff at the ideas of salvation and assurance, have wounded the faith and assurance of others, often by clever words in print, lectures, blogs, or websites.

Overconfidence is an especially sneaky troubler because it is so stealthy. People who made professions of faith and were given words of assurance sometimes drift away. If their lives bear no spiritual fruit for God, they should question their profession of faith. But sometimes instead they continue on, deceived by the troubler of overconfidence.

Until now this book has been negative. We have heard one problem story after another as we became acquainted with five troublers of the assurance of salvation. That was a painful but necessary first step that demands more steps. Accompany me as we journey into the Word of God to learn how God, in his immeasurable grace, assures believers that they know him. As we will see, God does so by making promises to us, by the Holy Spirit assuring us within, and by working in our lives. Come see how God's grace triumphs even over our troublers.

PART I

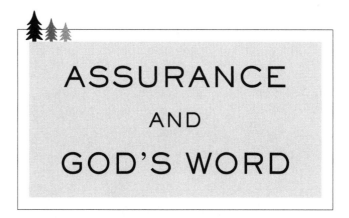

ASSURANCE

AND

GOD'S WORD

CHAPTER 2

ASSURANCE AND THE GOSPEL

God assures us in three main ways: by promising salvation in his Word, the Holy Spirit's ministering in our hearts, and God's working in our lives. Chapters 2–4 focus on the first of these. Through the gospel message, God assures us of his love and our eternal wellbeing. Anthony Hoekema neatly summarizes what is included in the gospel:

1. A presentation of the facts of the gospel and of the way of salvation
2. An invitation to come to Christ in repentance and faith
3. A promise of forgiveness and salvation[1]

Hoekema is right: the gospel includes God's promise to forgive our sins and to save us. And this promise brings assurance. The gospel itself is a substantial means that God uses graciously to assure his children that they belong to him. This chapter highlights six such gospel passages:

- John 3:16–18
- John 5:24
- Ephesians 2:1–9

- Hebrews 7:23–25
- Hebrews 10:11–14
- 1 Peter 1:3–5

JOHN 3:16-18

For God so loved the world that he gave his one and only Son, that whoever believes in him shall not perish but have eternal life. For God did not send his Son into the world to condemn the world, but to save the world through him. Whoever believes in him is not condemned, but whoever does not believe stands condemned already because they have not believed in the name of God's one and only Son.

In the Bible's most familiar verse we learn that God loved the world (John 3:16). This is the same world that other Scriptures declare opposed God (John 7:7; 15:18; 1 John 2:16). In a word, the world hated him. Yet he showed his love by giving his only Son; he sent him from heaven to earth to be born of the Virgin Mary, live a sinless life, and die for sinners. Consequently, all who trust him as Savior will not spend eternity in hell but will gain eternal life, starting now and continuing forever.

A Rescue Mission

John explains that the Father did not send his Son to condemn but to save (3:17). He came on a rescue mission. The Son brings judgment but only as a result of sinful opposition to his rescue mission. It is similar to missionaries who seek to bring salvation into a culture. An inescapable byproduct of their saving mission is judgment. Was it the missionaries' intention to condemn? Of course not. But because their proclamation of the gospel was met by unbelief, they inadvertently brought judgment. F. F. Bruce helpfully compares the different responses to the gospel to visitors viewing an art gallery:

In a gallery where artistic masterpieces are on display, it is not the masterpieces but the visitors that are on trial. The works which they view are not there to abide their question, but they reveal their own taste (or lack of it) by their reactions to what they see. The pop-star who was reported some years ago to have dismissed the Mona Lisa as a "load of rubbish" (except that he used a less polite word than "rubbish") did not tell us anything about the Mona Lisa; he told us much about himself. What is true in the aesthetic realm is equally true in the spiritual realm. The man who depreciates Christ, or thinks him unworthy of his allegiance, passes judgment on himself, not on Christ.[2]

The Son of God came to save, but an inescapable byproduct of his saving mission is judgment. Astoundingly, the Son's coming has brought to light the verdicts of the last day. Men and women do not need to wait for the final judgment to learn their eternal destinies. Those destinies are revealed now, depending upon people's relationship to Jesus Christ. This is bad news for those who reject Christ: "Whoever does not believe stands condemned already because they have not believed in the name of God's one and only Son" (v. 18). All who spurn Christ as he is offered in the gospel can know now the verdict of the last day. They do not need to wait to hear the divine Judge's verdict, for it has been rendered in advance—"condemnation"! In the flow of John's thought, this bad news is a part of the good news. God wants unbelievers to hear the word of condemnation and to turn to Christ in faith so that they might know a change of verdict.

Very Good News

Indeed, the announcement of the final verdicts ahead of time is very good news for all who trust Christ: "Whoever believes in him is not condemned" (v. 18). All who rely on Christ alone for salvation are assured now that God will not condemn them on the last day. The act of believing the gospel carries assurance because

it turns us away from ourselves to the Son of God, who alone
can save the lost. So John 3:16 is one of three verses that God put
together (vv. 16–18) to assure those who put their faith in Christ
for salvation. D. A. Carson is concise: "Thus the believer is not
condemned . . . and will not be condemned."[3]

JOHN 5:24

> Very truly I tell you, whoever hears my word and believes
> him who sent me has eternal life and will not be judged but
> has crossed over from death to life.

John's gospel uses words that are both simple and profound.
Sometimes this confuses readers. For example, Jesus speaks of
raising the dead at the end of the age: "Do not be amazed at this,
for a time is coming when all who are in their graves will hear
his voice and come out—those who have done what is good will
rise to live, and those who have done what is evil will rise to be
condemned" (John 5:28–29). Jesus, the Son of Man, will summon
the dead from their graves to meet their eternal destinies.

Spiritual Resurrection

So when Jesus uses similar language a few verses earlier, it
is natural to assume he is talking about the same thing—the resurrection on the last day: "Very truly I tell you, a time is coming
and has now come when the dead will hear the voice of the Son
of God and those who hear will live" (v. 25). At first blush this
sounds like Jesus is talking about raising the dead in his earthly
ministry. After all, this is what he did for the widow of Nain's
son, Jairus's daughter, and Lazarus. But this would be to arrive
at the wrong conclusion. Notice John's characteristic distinction
between "a time is coming, and has now come" (v. 25) and "a
time is coming" (v. 28). The latter expression points to something
that has not yet occurred, in this case the resurrection of the dead
on the last day. The former expression points to something that

has already occurred, in this case the spiritual resurrection of all who believe in Jesus in the present.

The immediately preceding verse confirms this conclusion. There Jesus says: "Very truly I tell you, whoever hears my word and believes him who sent me has eternal life and will not be judged but has crossed over from death to life" (v. 24). Those who hear Jesus's message and trust in him (and thereby the Father) move from one spiritual realm to another. They go from spiritual death to spiritual life. This is amazing! Taking Jesus at his word and putting trust in him as Savior means that you have been raised spiritually. This is like God's mighty resurrection of the body on the last day.

Faith in Jesus Brings Assurance

It follows, then, that believing in Jesus brings assurance of salvation. Everyone who experiences spiritual resurrection "does not come into judgment, but has passed from death to life" (v. 24 ESV) and will also experience "the resurrection of life" at the end of the age (v. 29 ESV). After Leon Morris explains John's teaching about the judgment of those who reject Christ, he draws a vital parallel:

> So with the man who has eternal life. His vindication is present in the here and now. He has already passed right out of the state of death, and has come into life. Though this is a present state it has future implications. The man who does not come into judgment will not come into judgment on the last great day either. . . . The saying points to his permanent safety. To have eternal life now is to be secure throughout eternity.[4]

Carson rightly discerns that John's language here "is virtually indistinguishable from . . . Paul's doctrine of justification: the believer does not come to the final judgment, but leaves the court already acquitted."[5] It is to Paul's teaching that we now turn.

EPHESIANS 2:1-9

As for you, you were dead in your transgressions and sins, in which you used to live when you followed the ways of this world and of the ruler of the kingdom of the air, the spirit who is now at work in those who are disobedient. All of us also lived among them at one time, gratifying the cravings of our flesh and following its desires and thoughts. Like the rest, we were by nature deserving of wrath. But because of his great love for us, God, who is rich in mercy, made us alive with Christ even when we were dead in transgressions—it is by grace you have been saved. And God raised us up with Christ and seated us with him in the heavenly realms in Christ Jesus, in order that in the coming ages he might show the incomparable riches of his grace, expressed in his kindness to us in Christ Jesus. For it is by grace you have been saved, through faith—and this is not from yourselves, it is the gift of God—not by works, so that no one can boast.

Like John, Paul ministers the gospel to believers to assure them of final salvation. Here he digs a deep hole out of which God's grace has dug all believers in Christ. First, before salvation we were spiritually dead, devoid of the life of God (v. 1). Second, we lived in the realm of sin and the world. Third, inadvertently, we followed the desires of Satan, who is active in unbelievers' lives (v. 2). Fourth, we lived for our sinful desires (v. 3). Fifth, "like the rest, we were by nature deserving of wrath" (v. 3)—that is, we and the whole human race deserved to have God's holy anger fall on us because of our rebellion against him.

Why does the apostle paint such a bleak picture of the human condition before salvation? For two reasons. It is a true picture: we were lost and unable to rescue ourselves, and God wants us to keep those facts in mind. And it makes us grateful for grace. Diamonds never shine more brightly than against the jeweler's purple cloth, so God's matchless grace shines all the more brightly against the background of our terrible plight.

A Stark Contrast

Verses 4–5 contrast sharply with what precedes: "But because of his great love for us, God, who is rich in mercy, made us alive with Christ even when we were dead in transgressions." Though we were as lost and helpless as the first three verses describe, God out of his abundant mercy loved us! Our salvation is certainly not because of any merit on our part. Rather, it is the result of God's "love . . . mercy . . . grace . . . [and] kindness" (vv. 4–5, 7).

How did God express his great compassion for us? He "made us alive with Christ" (v. 5). God caused those who were spiritually dead to come alive to himself. He did so "with Christ." That is, he spiritually united us to his Son so that his resurrection became ours. As Christ was raised from the dead, so we were made alive to God in Christ. Paul regards God's regenerating those dead in their sins as the epitome of grace. That's why he says next: "It is by grace you have been saved" (v. 5). Grace is God in his kindness rescuing those who cannot rescue themselves.

Seated with Christ in Heaven

God not only joined us spiritually to Christ in his resurrection, he also "raised us up with Christ and seated us with him in the heavenly realms in Christ Jesus" (v. 6). Scripture only says this here (though Colossians 3:3 implies it). What is God's purpose in this display of his marvelous grace in people's lives? He does so, Paul replies, "in order that in the coming ages he might show the incomparable riches of his grace, expressed in his kindness to us in Christ Jesus" (v. 7). God puts his church on display to demonstrate his grace to human beings and angels.

Again the apostle repeats a word of grace and expands it: "For it is by grace you have been saved, through faith—and this is not from yourselves, it is the gift of God—not by works, so that no one can boast." (vv. 8–9). Salvation is all of God and all of grace. Surely we have no reason to boast in ourselves and every reason to boast in God and his lovingkindness.

What does all this wonderful talk about God's grace have to do with assurance? First, we note with Frank Thielman that in this passage salvation is a *present* blessing enjoyed by believers: "Here salvation is something that is emphatically present for believers. They have already been made alive with Christ, already raised with him, and even already seated with him in the heavenly places. Their resurrection has, in some sense, already taken place."[6] Paul usually points to the future when he deals with salvation; he presents it as a glorious hope. Here, however, he emphasizes the present.

Still, how do his words exactly strengthen our assurance? F. F. Bruce tells us eloquently:

> That God has already seated his people with Christ in the heavenly realm is an idea unparalleled elsewhere in the Pauline corpus. It can best be understood as a statement of God's purpose for his people—a purpose which is so sure of fulfillment that it can be spoken of as having already taken place: "whom he justified, them he also glorified" (Rom. 8:30).[7]

The final salvation of God's people is so certain that in at least these two places—Ephesians 2:6 and Romans 8:30—he regards it as a *fait accompli*, a deed already done. God wants us to enjoy salvation now and to be confident that we cannot lose it. It is a permanent gift of his grace to his people. This good news should make us thankful, happy, and holy.

HEBREWS 7:23–25

> Now there have been many of those priests, since death prevented them from continuing in office; but because Jesus lives forever, he has a permanent priesthood. Therefore he is

able to save completely those who come to God through him, because he always lives to intercede for them.

The author of Hebrews often lauds Christ's superiority to his Old Testament counterparts, in this case the priests. Jesus is not a priest by heredity as were sons of Aaron. Instead, God's oath made him a priest, as predicted in Psalm 110:4 (cf. Heb. 7:20–21):

> The LORD has sworn
>> and will not change his mind:
> "You are a priest forever,
>> in the order of Melchizedek."

Mysteriously, Melchizedek appears out of nowhere in Genesis 14:18–20, as a priest of God Most High, and blesses Abraham, the father of Israel and its priesthood (because Aaron, the first high priest, descended from Abraham). Melchizedek disappears and reappears in the Old Testament in Psalm 110:4. Alone among New Testament writers, the writer to the Hebrews explains that Jesus is a priest according to the order of Melchizedek. This order has only two members: Melchizedek and Jesus.

Jesus also surpasses the Old Testament priests because his priesthood is not based on a tribal requirement. They had to be Aaron's descendants from the tribe of Levi. But Jesus's priesthood is "not on the basis of a regulation as to his ancestry but on the basis of the power of an indestructible life," namely his resurrection life (v. 16). Again, the writer appeals to Psalm 110:4, this time highlighting the word *forever*: "You are a priest forever" (v. 17).

Jesus's Permanent Priesthood

The author elaborates this point in verses 23–25. Because the Aaronic priesthood was hereditary, "there have been many of those priests, since death prevented them from continuing in office" (v. 23). When the high priest died, he would be succeeded by his son, and when his son died, by his son's son, and so forth.

Contrary to the Old Testament priests, "because Jesus lives forever, he has a permanent priesthood" (v. 24). Because Jesus arose from the dead after he died on the cross, he does not need a replacement; his priesthood is eternal.

Jesus's permanent priesthood, based on his death and resurrection, provides strong encouragement to believers: "because Jesus lives forever, he has a permanent priesthood. Therefore he is able to save completely those who come to God through him, because he always lives to intercede for them" (vv. 24–25). The living Christ, our great High Priest, "has a permanent priesthood." His once-for-all sacrifice on the cross saves us from the beginning to the end of the Christian life. Because he arose from the dead he is able to keep us saved. He saves "completely" everyone who comes to him for salvation (v. 25). "Completely" means not only "forever" but "absolutely."[8] Jesus saves in every way that salvation can be conceived. His people are safe in his care. F. F. Bruce exults, "His once-completed self-offering is utterly acceptable and efficacious; His contact with the Father is immediate and unbroken; His priestly ministry on His people's behalf is never-ending; and therefore the salvation which He secures to them is absolute."[9]

Jesus's Intercession

The writer to the Hebrews adds another key detail; he says that the ascended Christ "always lives to intercede for them" (v. 25). Christ's heavenly intercession is often misunderstood. We should not envision him as pleading with the Father on our behalf. He does not need to plead, for "after he had provided purification for sins" the Son "sat down at the right hand of the Majesty in heaven" (Heb. 1:3). This indicates that the Father accepts his Son's sacrifice as complete, perfect, and efficacious. The result? Believers can have confidence of their final salvation. As Philip Hughes explains,

> How can we who draw near to God through Christ fail to be eternally secure in view of the fact not only that *he always*

lives but also that as our ever living priest he never ceases *to make intercession* for us in the heavenly sanctuary? With him as our intercessor, supporting us by his strength and surrounding us with his love, there is no force that can daunt or overpower us (cf. Phil 4:13; Rom. 8:37).[10]

HEBREWS 10:11-14

Day after day every priest stands and performs his religious duties; again and again he offers the same sacrifices, which can never take away sins. But when this priest had offered for all time one sacrifice for sins, he sat down at the right hand of God, and since that time he waits for his enemies to be made his footstool. For by one sacrifice he has made perfect forever those who are being made holy.

Again the writer to the Hebrews sharply contrasts Christ and Old Testament priests. He begins: "Day after day every priest stands and performs his religious duties; again and again he offers the same sacrifices, which can never take away sins" (v. 11). In his next statement (v. 12), he draws five contrasts with this one. First, "every priest" in the Old Testament contrasts with the *one* Christ. The person, and therefore the work, of Jesus is absolutely unique. Second, the former priests stand and Christ "sat down." Their standing indicated that their work was not completed. His sitting indicates that his work is indeed finished. His sacrifice makes an end to all sacrifices. Third, Old Testament priests offer multiple sacrifices whereas Christ provides "one sacrifice for sins." It is one sacrifice because it is perfect and perfectly accepted in heaven. There is no longer a need for sacrifices. Fourth, the former priests offered "again and again . . . the same sacrifices," and Christ "offered for all time one sacrifice for sins." Because his sacrifice is perfect, it is non-repeatable. It avails for the salvation of all God's people of all time. Fifth, the Old Testament priests' offerings could "never take away sins," and Christ's sacrifice did that very thing, as verse 14 reveals. His sacrifice brings final and complete forgiveness. Therefore, it brings believers great assurance, as we will see below.

The Great and Final High Priest

Christ's priestly ministry far outweighs that of his Old Testament predecessors. There are two main points to these contrasts that display the superiority of Christ's priestly ministry. The writer to the Hebrews extols both the person and work of Christ. First, he praises him as the only Mediator between God and human beings (1 Tim. 2:5). Second, he rejoices in Christ's unique accomplishment. His death is the perfect and final sacrifice for sins.

Christ offered himself "once for all" and "for all time" (vv. 10, 12). These expressions point to the uniqueness of Christ's saving death (7:27; 9:12, 26, 28). There never has been or will be anything like it. It secured "eternal redemption" (9:12). As Mediator of the new covenant, his death brings "the promised eternal inheritance" to his people (9:15). The saving effects of Christ's atonement know no end. He came "to do away with sin by the sacrifice of himself" (9:26). His people, then, can have assurance of forgiveness in this life and the life to come.

The contrasts between Christ's priesthood and the Old Testament's also underscore God's intention to give confidence to his people and to motivate them to continue in the faith. The writer makes this application in verse 14: "For by one sacrifice he has made perfect forever those who are being made holy." These words are stunning! God forgives us because of what Jesus did for us, and he forgives us *forever*. Now, of course, we are far from perfect in our thoughts, words, and actions. But in God's sight we have been made holy forever!

Assurance and Motivation

Such exalted words bring great assurance to all who know Christ. At the same time they motivate us to live for him. Hebrews is written to a community of professed Hebrew Christians who are being pressured to deny Christ in order to escape persecution.

The writer exhorts them frequently to persevere. Here he does so by implication. "By one sacrifice" Christ has perfected for all time *"those who are being made holy."* The people who have been perfected in God's sight are identifiable—they are growing in grace and being made progressively holy.

The remainder of verse 14 is remarkable. God's people striving to be "made holy" is not the basis of his acceptance of them. He accepts them because of Christ's "one sacrifice." But neither may they take it easy. If they really know Christ, they work hard, in his power, at holiness. God assures his people, according to Hebrews 10:14, both by his promise, which is based on Christ's unique atonement, and by urging them to persevere in faith and holiness.

Bruce underlines the great confidence of final salvation that believers can enjoy: "The sacrifice of Christ has purified His people from the moral defilement of sin, and assured them of permanent maintenance in a right relation to God."[11]

1 PETER 1:3–5

Praise be to the God and Father of our Lord Jesus Christ! In his great mercy he has given us new birth into a living hope through the resurrection of Jesus Christ from the dead, and into an inheritance that can never perish, spoil or fade. This inheritance is kept in heaven for you, who through faith are shielded by God's power until the coming of the salvation that is ready to be revealed in the last time.

Ordinarily when we think of God's giving new life to those who are spiritually dead (regeneration), we think of the Holy Spirit, and rightly so. The Spirit plays a prominent role in regeneration, as the following passages show:

The wind blows wherever it pleases. You hear its sound, but you cannot tell where it comes from or where it is going. So it is with everyone born of the Spirit. (John 3:8)

The Spirit gives life; the flesh counts for nothing. The words I have spoken to you—they are full of the Spirit and life. (John 6:63)

But when the kindness and love of God our Savior appeared, he saved us, . . . through the washing of rebirth and renewal by the Holy Spirit. (Titus 3:4–5)

The Spirit is the person of the Trinity who quickens us; he makes us come alive to God and to spiritual things. Peter shows that the Father and the Son also are active in regeneration. The apostle adores the Father: "Praise be to the God and Father of our Lord Jesus Christ! In his great mercy he has given us new birth into a living hope through the resurrection of Jesus Christ from the dead" (v. 3). The Father in his mercy causes regeneration; he is the author of the new birth. The Son plays a role too. We are regenerated "through the resurrection of Jesus Christ from the dead." Christ's resurrection provides the power for regeneration. His resurrection life is the basis for our new life.

In sum, the Father plans for us to receive spiritual life. He does so based on the Son overcoming death in his resurrection. Then the Spirit applies the Father's plan and the Son's work to individual lives when he causes them to be born again (regenerated).

A Grand Goal

The Trinity's work of regeneration has a grand goal: it provides believers an inheritance. Peter lavishly describes this inheritance. It "can never perish, spoil or fade. This inheritance is kept in heaven for [Christians]" (v. 4). This inheritance, unlike any on earth, cannot be corrupted, tarnished by sin, lose its beauty, or be forfeited. Put positively, it will retain its value, its purity, and its luster, and it will last forever.

Because Peter began his letter by describing Christians in terms regularly used to describe Israel ("elect exiles of the Dispersion," v. 1 ESV), he probably implies a contrast here between

Christians' heavenly inheritance and that of Old Testament Israel. Wayne Grudem summarizes,

> The "inheritance" of the New Covenant Christian is thus shown to be far superior to the earthly inheritance of the people of Israel in the land of Canaan. That earthly land was not "kept" for them, but was *taken from them* in the exile, and later by Roman occupation. Even while they possessed the land, it produced rewards that *decayed*, rewards whose glory *faded* away. The beauty of the land's holiness before God was repeatedly *defiled* by sin.[12]

Peter's last description of our inheritance is most important for the topic of assurance. Our inheritance is "kept in heaven for you, who through faith are shielded by God's power until the coming of the salvation that is ready to be revealed in the last time" (vv. 4–5). Our heavenly inheritance is reserved for us. God has prepared a place in his kingdom for each of his sons and daughters.

What is the significance of Peter saying that Christians' inheritance is "kept in heaven" (v. 4)? Thomas Schreiner answers: "The passive of the word 'kept' (*teteremenen*) is a divine passive, referring to God as the one who reserves the inheritance for believers. Peter emphasized in the strongest possible terms the security and certainty of the reward awaiting believers."[13]

We Are Kept

Not only is believers' inheritance kept by God; the believers themselves are kept by him as well. They are those "who through faith are shielded by God's power" (v. 5). True believers in Jesus will not fail to obtain their heavenly inheritance. That inheritance is referred to as "the salvation" in verse 5. Salvation in Scripture is past, present, and future. God has saved his people once for all in the past: "By grace you have been saved through faith" (Eph. 2:8). He saves them in the present by affording them mercy and grace when they cry out to him: "Let us then approach God's throne of grace with confidence, so that we may receive mercy and find grace to help us in our time of need" (Heb. 4:16). Most often Scripture says God will yet save his people from their sins: "But in keeping with his promise we are looking forward to a new heaven and a new earth, where righteousness dwells" (2 Peter 3:13).

Peter has the future tense of salvation in view in 1 Peter 1:5. His readers are among those "who through faith are shielded by God's power until the coming of the salvation that is ready to be revealed in the last time." God, by his power, guards his people for final salvation. The apostle uses a military metaphor to speak of Christians, as Peter Davids clarifies:

> There is a conscious balance between God's action in heaven, protecting their future, and his action on earth, protecting them in the present. The picture is that of a fortress or military camp. They are within. Outside the evil forces are assaulting them. But on the perimeter is the overwhelming force of "the power of God." He it is who protects them. . . . They may seem vulnerable to themselves, and indeed in themselves they are, but God's goodness and protection surrounds them. He will do the protecting.[14]

God guards his people in salvation through a process, and God does so "through faith," that is, he uses the instrumentality of faith to keep believers saved. Make no mistake, "believers must exercise faith to receive final salvation," but this is not a self-help program. "God's power protects us because his power is the means by which our faith is sustained," as Schreiner says.[15]

CONCLUSION

In chapter 1, we heard Erica's story (pp. 17–18). Her father's rejection hindered her ability to believe that God loved and accepted her. Erica and those with similar struggles might benefit from this chapter's message. We heard a chorus of biblical authors strengthen assurance by highlighting God's promises to save and keep his people. Erica needs to hear again and again the message of God's love for us and the fact that he accepts us in Christ. All six passages contain this message. Several of them explicitly sing of God's mercy and love:

> For *God so loved* the world that he gave his one and only Son. (John 3:16)

> But because of *his great love* for us, God, who is *rich in mercy*, made us alive with Christ even when we were dead in transgressions—it is by *grace* you have been saved. . . . in order that in the coming ages he might show the *incomparable riches of his grace*, expressed in *his kindness* to us in Christ Jesus. For it is by *grace* you have been saved. (Eph. 2:4–8)

> Praise be to the God and Father of our Lord Jesus Christ! In his great *mercy* he has given us new birth into a living hope. (1 Peter 1:3)

In fact, halfway through college, Erica heard a sermon on the parable of the prodigal son. The message emphasized the father's love and grace and applied it to our relationship with God. It's unusual that one sermon so dramatically changes someone's life, but that's what happened with Erica. She began to study and memorize Scriptures on God's grace, mercy, and love. For the first time in her Christian life, she felt accepted by God and had a relationship with God as her Father.

After college, she went into family counseling, working with troubled teens. Understanding and applying God the Father's grace and acceptance is a critical part of her life and message. Today Erica has a good marriage, and two grown children to whom she has been an attentive and loving parent, the opposite of what she experienced from her father.

Since the gospel includes God's promise to forgive us, it brings assurance of salvation. The gospel proclaims that our heavenly Father loves and accepts us into his family when we trust his Son.

CHAPTER 3

ASSURANCE AND PRESERVATION IN JOHN

God assures us by his Word, promising to save and keep all who believe in his Son. The previous chapter argued that the gospel brings assurance. This chapter concentrates on two writings of the apostle John, his gospel and first epistle. We begin with the latter because of its clear witness to the fact that God wants believers in his Son to have assurance of salvation.

GOD WANTS US TO HAVE ASSURANCE

Before setting forth abundant evidence from Scripture that God saves and keeps his people, we review the fact that God wants his saints to have assurance. Previously we studied 1 John's purpose statement in 5:11–13: "And this is the testimony: God has given us eternal life, and this life is in his Son. Whoever has the Son has life; whoever does not have the Son of God does not have life. I write these things to you who believe in the name of the Son of God so that you may know that you have eternal life." Contrary to what many say, God wants those who trust Christ for salvation to have confidence that they belong to him, to "know that" they "have eternal life."

This chapter emphasizes the apostle John's presentation of how the Word of God assures us. By "the Word of God" I mean the Bible, especially its promise of salvation, its message of good news, the gospel. Because I began with the purpose statement of 1 John, I will continue to treat assurance passages in that epistle before turning our attention to the Gospel of John.

- 1 John 2:18–19
- 1 John 5:18
- John 6:35, 37–40, 44
- John 10:27–30
- John 17:9–12, 15, 24

1 JOHN 2:18-19

Dear children, this is the last hour; and as you have heard that the antichrist is coming, even now many antichrists have come. This is how we know it is the last hour. They went out from us, but they did not really belong to us. For if they had belonged to us, they would have remained with us; but their going showed that none of them belonged to us.[1]

At first glance 1 John 2:18–19 says little about God's granting assurance based on his promise of salvation. Closer inspection, however, reveals this passage to do that very thing. John warns of a breach in the community caused by "antichrists." He defines an *antichrist* as "whoever denies that Jesus is the Christ," which amounts to "denying the Father and the Son" (v. 22). He contrasts one antichrist figure and "many antichrists." The former is still future, while the latter are already present in the churches. The antichrists are the false teachers who have done spiritual harm to the recipients of John's letter. Because of the presence of the antichrists, John concludes that the end times are upon us: "Dear children, this is the last hour; and as you have heard that the antichrist is coming, even now many antichrists have come."

That it is already the final hour adds urgency to John's next words: "They went out from us, but they did not really belong to us. For if they had belonged to us, they would have remained with us; but their going showed that none of them belonged to us" (v. 19).

The antichrists did not work their evil from without the community but from within. They joined the churches to which John writes. Later, however, they left the churches and in so doing showed their true identity. Their leaving, John teaches, exposes the fact that the antichrists were not authentic children of God. Robert Yarbrough clarifies:

> People have left the community, in John's estimation, because in one or more fundamental respects they were not truly part of it. . . . Those who have departed condemn themselves; . . . Such persons are outside the pale of Christ's followers as a result of their willful apostasy. . . . Quite simply, these people did not see fit to *remain* within the apostolic parameters that for John were inclusive of true Christians.[2]

The false teachers were guilty of apostasy. They defected from a faith formerly professed. Although they were among believers and appeared to belong to Christ and the church, they did not truly belong. Their leaving revealed their true identity, as John Stott concludes: "Only on the final day of separation will the wheat and the tares be completely revealed. Meanwhile, some are shown up in their true colours by their defection."[3] Among them will be the antichrists whom John denounces.

Indeed, John speaks plainly, "For if they had belonged to us, they would have remained with us." If the false teachers had been true believers, they would have remained in the church.[4] D. E. Hiebert explains the sense of the Greek construction used here: "For if they were from us (but they weren't), they would have remained with us (but they didn't)."[5] John's message is clear: The false teachers did not belong and therefore deserted. Authentic believers, however, persevere in Christian fellowship.

Genuine Faith Perseveres

Ironically, John's warning to the churches about false teachers gives true believers assurance of salvation. John writes to protect his readers from potential despondency. They should not despair when the false teachers desert them because this desertion distinguishes true believers from false ones. Because God preserves his own for final salvation, genuine Christians persevere to the end in faith. By implication, apostates are false Christians. As D. A. Carson points out,

> The same stance is reflected in 1 John 2:19. Those who have seceded from the church are described in telling terms: "They went out from us, but they did not really belong to us. For if they had belonged to us, they would have remained with us; but their going showed that none of them belonged to us." In other words, genuine faith, by definition, perseveres; where there is no perseverance, by definition the faith cannot be genuine.[6]

Genuine faith perseveres. True believers do not merely make an initial profession of faith in Jesus. They do so and then continue to trust him for salvation. They go on with him. They often struggle and sometimes doubt. But they never fall away "totally and finally."[7] Genuine Christians are not like Jason, whose story in chapter 1 illustrates overconfidence (see pp. 28–29). Jason stepped forward at an evangelist's meeting, repeated a prayer, and was told he was safe forever. True children of God do not, like Jason, make a profession and then give no thought to the kind of life God wants them to live. Rather, they truly believe the gospel and keep on believing it—through thick and thin, the rest of their lives. The promise of salvation, which they cling to, assures them that God loves them, Christ died to rescue them, and they are among God's children. Because the gospel is true and because they really believe it, God works in their lives as a confirmation of his love. God is kind. He distinguishes true and false faith. The latter falls away. The former endures. We continue to believe God's promise of salvation. We keep going to church with God's people, where the Word of God is honored and proclaimed. And these faithful practices give us confidence that God belongs to us and we belong to him.

1 JOHN 5:18

We know that anyone born of God does not continue to sin; the One who was born of God keeps them safe, and the evil one cannot harm them.

John offers these words of assurance when he encourages his readers to live for Christ: "We know that anyone born of God does not continue to sin" (v. 18). John teaches that all whom the Father has regenerated do not practice sin the way they did before regeneration. John does not teach perfectionism; Christians still sin (1:8, 10). But they also confess their sins, take forgiveness and cleansing from God, and keep pursuing godliness (1:9; 2:1–2). Why? Because Christ protects them: "The One who was born of God keeps them safe, and the evil one cannot harm them" (5:18).

The Son Keeps Us Safe

"The One who was born of God" does not refer to believers but to Christ, the unique Son of God.[8] John implies that regenerate persons persevere in holiness because the unique Son "keeps them safe." Ultimately, Christ's protection produces godliness.

Christ also shields Christians from the devil. Because Christ protects us, "the evil one does not touch" us (v. 18 ESV). *Touch* in this context means "touching" or "laying hold" to the point of doing harm.[9] The devil is stronger than we are and seeks to harm us: "Your enemy the devil prowls around like a roaring lion looking for someone to devour" (1 Peter 5:8). One reason the evil one does not "devour" believers is because Christ guards them from falling into ruinous sin. As John Stott explains,

The devil, *the evil one*, is maliciously active. Strong and subtle, he is more than a match for [the believer alone].

> But the Son of God came to destroy the devil's work (3:8),
> and if he *keeps . . . safe* the Christian, the devil will not be
> able to *harm* him. . . . The devil does not touch the Christian
> because the Son keeps him, and so, because the Son keeps
> him, the Christian does not persist in sin.[10]

Unlike the world that "lies in the power of the evil one," believers
"are from God" (1 John 5:19 ESV); they have been begotten by
the Father and belong to him. As a result his Son protects them
from sin and Satan. John thus gives us a powerful word of assurance. Jesus not only saves his own once and for all. He protects
them so they are not overwhelmed by sin or destroyed by the
devil. He is a wonderful Savior who assures his people with such
warm words of encouragement.

The Bible doesn't give us cure-alls that heal problems on contact,
but it does meet us in our struggles with real help. This verse in
1 John provides such help for people like Steve, whom we met in
chapter 1 (pp. 22–23), whose sensitive hearts and strong emotions are
sometimes a blessing and sometimes a curse. By his own admission,
some days Steve does not feel like God loves him. The knowledge that
Jesus shields us from the worst effects of our sin and from Satan's
darts can strengthen all of us, especially "Steves" and "Stephanies,"
for the battles we face. Such knowledge will not make our problems
disappear, but it can fortify us to face our problems with less fear.
This single verse, 1 John 5:18, will not insulate us from all temptation.
But it can help us endure temptation when it comes.

Jesus's powerful words in the Gospel of John have given confidence of salvation to multitudes of believers over the centuries.
We turn to some of them now.

JOHN 6:35, 37–40, 44

Then Jesus declared, "I am the bread of life. Whoever comes
to me will never go hungry, and whoever believes in me will
never be thirsty. . . . All those the Father gives me will come

to me, and whoever comes to me I will never drive away. For
I have come down from heaven not to do my will but to do
the will of him who sent me. And this is the will of him who
sent me, that I shall lose none of all those he has given me,
but raise them up at the last day. For my Father's will is that
everyone who looks to the Son and believes in him shall have
eternal life, and I will raise them up at the last day. . . . No
one can come to me unless the Father who sent me draws
them, and I will raise them up at the last day."

After feeding five thousand by multiplying loaves and fish,
Jesus preaches his famous bread of life sermon. We need to
understand John's vocabulary to appreciate his message. In verse
35, Jesus makes "coming to" him parallel to "believing in" him:
"I am the bread of life. Whoever *comes to me* will never go hungry, and whoever *believes in me* will never be thirsty." The two
expressions are synonymous. To come to Jesus is one way John
speaks of putting faith in him.

Another piece of distinctive vocabulary is Jesus's use of the
Father "giving" people to him: "all those the Father *gives* me" (v. 37)
means all those the Father chose for salvation. The Father giving
people to the Son is one of the ways John talks about election.[11]
John also talks about the Father "drawing" people to Jesus: "No
one can come to me unless the Father who sent me draws them"
(v. 44). John's use of *drawing* approximates Paul's use of *calling*,
or effectively summoning people to Jesus through the gospel. The
Father draws his people to him, bringing them to Jesus for salvation.

Jesus Will Never Reject Us

We are now better situated to understand Jesus's message of
assurance. When Jesus says, "All those the Father gives me *will
come* to me" (John 6:37), he means all whom the Father chose
will certainly believe in him. Although some claim that election
is based on faith, John teaches the opposite—faith is the result of
election. Jesus adds comforting words: "Whoever comes to me I

will never drive away" (v. 37). Jesus promises to keep all those who trust him for salvation. He will never reject those who come to him in saving faith. God keeps his people saved forever, and another name for that is *preservation.*

Jesus says that he came from heaven to earth to do the Father's will. Then he adds, "And this is the will of him who sent me, that I shall lose none of all those he has given me, but raise them up at the last day" (v. 39). By saving and keeping his people, Jesus fulfills the Father's plan. Furthermore, Jesus promises to keep all believers saved until the day he raises them from the dead to enjoy life with him and the Father on the new earth forever. Jesus grants all believers eternal life now and resurrection to life at the end of the age. Jesus repeats, "For my Father's will is that everyone who looks to the Son and believes in him shall have eternal life, and I will raise them up at the last day" (v. 40).

Again Jesus affirms that the people of God are safe in his care. "No one can come to me unless the Father who sent me draws them, and I will raise them up at the last day" (v. 44). Only those drawn (called inwardly) by the Father believe in Jesus. And Jesus promises to raise all believers for final salvation.

The Father and Son Work Together

All in all, John paints a beautiful picture of harmony between the Father and Son in salvation, and his picture fortifies assurance. Here is a summary:

- The Father gives people to the Son (election; John 6:37).
- The Father draws them to the Son (calling; John 6:44).
- They come to the Son for salvation (faith; John 6:37, 40, 44).
- The Son keeps them saved (preservation; John 6:37, 39).
- The Son will raise them to life on the last day
  (resurrection; John 6:39, 40, 44).

The Father and Son work in unison. The Father chooses people and draws them to faith in the Son. They believe in him and are saved. The Son preserves them and will raise them for eternal life. The Father and Son work in harmony to save and keep Christians.

Because the Father and the Son work harmoniously in salvation, there is continuity for those who are saved. The people the Father gives to the Son and draws to him are the same people who come to the Son, whom the Son saves and keeps, and whom he will raise on the last day. The identity of those God saves is constant from the beginning of salvation to the end. This is significant because it draws attention to God's promises to keep his people saved. Because of the harmonious work of the Father and Son, all believers are safe and will not be cast out, will not be lost, but will be raised for life (vv. 37, 39).

Jesus's promises are more impressive when set out:

All those the Father gives me will come to me, and whoever comes to me I will never drive away. (v. 37)

And this is the will of him who sent me, that I shall lose none of all those he has given me, but raise them up at the last day. (v. 39)

For my Father's will is that everyone who looks to the Son and believes in him shall have eternal life, and I will raise them up at the last day. (v. 40)

No one can come to me unless the Father who sent me draws them, and I will raise them up at the last day. (v. 44)

In plain words, Jesus repeatedly teaches our preservation—he will keep us for salvation on the last day. We are overwhelmed by his magnificent grace. As we grow in Christ, he shows us more of our weaknesses, and this in turn makes us more thankful for his grace, which saves and keeps us. Thomas Schreiner and Ardel Caneday are correct: "We know that we are prone to wander, but we have the promise that Jesus will never lose us, that the work he began he will also complete on the day of our resurrection."[12]

Jesus's message offers help to those who struggle because of their background or life experiences. Remember Erica, from the first chapter (pp. 17–18), who suffered rejection from a cold and distant father and struggled to believe that God accepted her? Thankfully, Erica let Jesus's words "remain in" her (John 15:7), and learned to hear his voice and follow him (10:27). His assuring words found a place in her heart and changed her life. Though most of us will never know the disappointments that Erica knew, all of us will experience some disappointment, but Jesus does not disappoint (1 Peter 2:6). He rescues and keeps his people and wants them to rest in his love and keeping power.

JOHN 10:27–30

My sheep listen to my voice; I know them, and they follow me. I give them eternal life, and they shall never perish; no one will snatch them out of my hand. My Father, who has given them to me, is greater than all; no one can snatch them out of my Father's hand. I and the Father are one.

This is one of the two most famous passages in the New Testament about God keeping his people saved (the other is Romans 8:28–39). It appears as a part of Jesus's Good Shepherd discourse. The Lord blasts the unfaithful shepherds of Old Testament Israel (Ezek. 34:1–10) who do not care for their flock but let them stray to become food for wild animals. Jesus also speaks against the "thieves and robbers" who come "only to steal and kill and destroy" (John 10:8, 10). He is referring to the leaders of Israel who refuse to accept him as their Messiah and prevent the people from doing so, as is shown by their mistreatment of the blind man whom Jesus healed (John 9). Jesus, the Good Shepherd, replaces these unfaithful shepherds both old and new. He loves the sheep and gives himself up for them. Five times he speaks of laying down his life for his sheep (John 10:11, 15, 17, 18 [2x]). He lays down his life, in crucifixion, and he is able to "take it up again" in resurrection (vv. 17–18).

Some Jewish leaders challenge Jesus: "How long will you keep us in suspense? If you are the Messiah, tell us plainly" (v. 24). They did not say this sincerely but only to test him, as his reply reveals: "I did tell you, but you do not believe. The works I do in my Father's name testify about me" (v. 25). The Jewish opponents do not reject Jesus because of a lack of evidence. His words and deeds abundantly testify to his being "the Christ, the Son of God" (20:30 ESV).

His opponents are culpable for their unbelief but Jesus appeals to a more profound reason: "You do not believe because you are not my sheep" (10:26). Of course it is true that they are not part of his flock because they do not believe in him; John frequently regards unbelief as blameworthy. But Jesus doesn't say they are not his because they don't believe. Instead, he says *they do not believe because they are not his.* This is one of John's pictures of election, of God's choosing his people for salvation. According to John, God's people have a prior identity that is shown by their believing in Jesus. Verse 26 also teaches that those who are not God's people have a prior identity that is revealed in relation to Jesus. They reject him and thereby show they do not belong to God's people.

Our primary concern, however, is with Jesus's people, his sheep. In contrast to those who spurn him, the sheep listen to him; they believe in him. Furthermore, he knows them personally and they follow him, that is, they obey his commands (v. 27). The words concerning preservation that follow are as important as any in Scripture. Jesus says, "I give them eternal life, and they shall never perish; no one will snatch them out of my hand. My Father, who has given them to me, is greater than all; no one can snatch them out of my Father's hand. I and the Father are one" (vv. 28–30).

Early and often in his gospel, John pictures Jesus as the giver of eternal life. John announces that even before the eternal Word became a man, he, in whom alone eternal life resides, created all things and thereby gave them life (1:3–4). Consequently, it does not surprise us that the Word who became flesh gives physical and spiritual life to sinners in need. After healing the legs of a man paralyzed for thirty-eight years, Jesus says, "For just as the Father raises the dead and gives them life, even so the Son gives life to whom he is pleased to give it" (5:21). In addition, John portrays Jesus as "the bread of life" (6:35), "the resurrection and the life" (11:25), and "the way, and the truth and the life" (14:6). All these images present Jesus as the Life-Giver.

"They Shall Never Perish"

It is appropriate, therefore, for Jesus to proclaim that eternal life is his gift to his sheep: "I give them eternal life" (10:28). In contrast to those who are not his sheep, who reject him, and are rejected by God, Jesus's sheep receive the gift of eternal life from their Good Shepherd. Jesus utters the staggering words, "They shall never perish" (v. 28). English translations can hardly communicate the force of the original Greek. Daniel B. Wallace, the author of a respected Greek grammar, explains:

> Emphatic negation is indicated by *ou me* plus the *aorist subjunctive*. . . . This is the strongest way to negate something in Greek. . . . *Ou me* rules out even the idea as being a possibility. . . . Emphatic negation is found primarily in the reported sayings of Jesus. . . . As well, a *soteriological* theme is frequently found in such statements, especially in John: what is negatived is the possibility of the loss of salvation.[13]

John 10:28 is among the examples that Wallace lists. He translates: "I give them eternal life, and they will *not at all* perish."[14] Jesus most emphatically states that those to whom he gives eternal life will never be cast into hell. Positively said, they will surely gain final salvation. Jesus, the Savior of the world, makes one of the strongest statements of God's preservation of his people in all of Scripture. It is difficult to maintain that some of the sheep will perish (by losing salvation) when Jesus categorically says they will not.

Safe in the Hands of the Father and the Son

Jesus's next words make his statement even weightier: "No one will snatch them out of my hand" (v. 28). Jesus, the Good Shepherd, holds his lambs in his arms, and no enemy can open his strong grip. The word *snatch* speaks of a violent attempt to tear the sheep from their Shepherd. The people of God are safe in the love and protection of their powerful Savior.

Jesus continues, "My Father, who has given them to me, is greater than all, no one can snatch them out of my Father's hand" (v. 29). Here John teaches both the deity and humanity of the incarnate Son. Jesus, acting as only God can, gives eternal life as a gift. No creature, whether angel or human, can do that; only God himself bestows life. John also teaches that in becoming a man the Son of God subordinates himself to his Father. This is what Jesus means when he says: "My Father . . . is greater than all." Both the Son of God and God the Father have a solid grip on their flock. The sheep are safe in the formidable arms of the Father and the Son.

Jesus's words, "I and the Father are one" (v. 30), are often misunderstood as explicitly teaching that the Father and the Son share God's essence. That certainly is a biblical truth (Heb. 1:3 teaches it), but it is not directly taught here. Instead, according to the preceding context, Jesus indicates that he and the Father are one in preserving the people of God. Jesus gives the sheep eternal life and they will never perish. Why? He and the Father hold the sheep in their power, and no one can take them away. Jesus means that he and the Father are one in keeping the people of God safe for final salvation. John 10:30 indeed affirms the deity of Christ, and it does so by crediting Jesus with a work that only God can perform—preservation.

It is no wonder this passage is famous as a proof text for eternal security. Three times, Jesus asserts that his sheep are safe. First, after saying he gives them life, he categorically says that they will never perish. Second, he declares the sheep safe in his mighty arms, saying that no one can snatch them away from him. Third, he adds that the Father also holds, protects, and keeps the sheep safely in his powerful arms as well.

D. A. Carson concludes, "The focus is . . . on Jesus's power: *no-one can snatch them out of my hand*, not the marauding wolf (v. 12), not the thieves and robbers (vv. 1, 8), not anyone."[15] Leon Morris sums up John's teaching in 10:28–30: "It is one of the precious things about the Christian faith that our continuance in eternal life depends not on our feeble hold on Christ, but on His firm grip on us."[16] The sheep are in the safest place imaginable—in the almighty arms of the Son and the Father.

Help for Stress, Sensitive Hearts, and Discouragement

These truths offer a tremendous help to Christians wrestling with various troublers to their souls. I do not belittle those under great stress like Elijah (1 Kings 18). Nevertheless, when we have rested and can look back on extremely stressful situations that we have survived, it is comforting to know that the everlasting, strong arms of the Father and the Son have been supporting and continue to support us. We do not keep ourselves saved. God preserves us, and as a result, we love and obey him.

Jesus gives eternal life as a gift to his people and declares that they will *never* perish. This offers help to those with sensitive hearts who tend to base their status with God on their feelings. Once more, I do not look down on my brothers and sisters who suffer from great discouragement. I have experienced a taste of it and found it bitter! It is debilitating. But even when we are down, we dare not give up. Once more Scripture offers no magic wand. But there is help—even if we can only receive it over time—from the healing words of Jesus, the Good Shepherd of the sheep. We are all sheep, and we do foolish and self-destructive things.

But still Jesus loves and keeps us in his arms, and that means a lot. May God grant us grace and peace, with the result that Jesus's love and keeping will mean even more to us.

JOHN 17:9-12, 15, 24

> I pray for them. I am not praying for the world, but for those you have given me, for they are yours. All I have is yours, and all you have is mine. And glory has come to me through them. I will remain in the world no longer, but they are still in the world, and I am coming to you. Holy Father, protect them by the power of your name, the name you gave me, so that they may be one as we are one. While I was with them, I protected them and kept them safe by that name you gave me. None has been lost except the one doomed to destruction so that Scripture would be fulfilled. . . . My prayer is not that you take them out of the world but that you protect them from the evil one. . . . Father, I want those you have given me to be with me where I am, and to see my glory, the glory you have given me because you loved me before the creation of the world.

Did you ever wonder what Jesus is praying as he intercedes for us in heaven? (Rom. 8:34; Heb. 7:25)? The Lord gives us a pretty good idea in his prayer to the Father in John 17. The traditional breakdown seems correct: Jesus prays for himself (vv. 1–5), his eleven disciples (vv. 6–19), and future believers (vv. 20–26). Although he makes many requests, four stand out. He prays for Christians' unity (vv. 11, 21, 22, 23), holiness (vv. 17, 19), witness to the world (vv. 18, 21, 23), and preservation (vv. 11–12, 15, 24). We are especially interested in the last. Four times in John 17, Jesus speaks of preservation, of God keeping believers saved.

Jesus does not pray for the world but for those the Father gave him, those the Father chose (v. 9). These people belong to the Father and the Son. Surprisingly in light of the disciples' struggles,

Jesus says that he is glorified in them (vv. 9–10). He then says, "I will remain in the world no longer . . . and I am coming to you" (v. 11), indicating that he is so resolute that in his mind's eye his work on earth is completed (see v. 4). This is typical of his stance in this prayer. Even though it occurs before his death, resurrection, and ascension, he prays as if he has already returned to the Father in heaven. Let's look more closely at these four prayers.

Prayer 1: That the Father Himself Uphold Believers (v. 11)

Though Jesus prays as if he has returned to the Father, his disciples remain in the world. Accordingly, he prays, "Holy Father, protect them by the power of your name—the name you gave me" (v. 11).[17] The context illumines Jesus's request. Because Jesus is sovereign over all human beings, he gives eternal life to those the Father gave him (v. 2). Jesus defines eternal life: it is knowing the Father and the Son (v. 3). He adds that he revealed the Father to those he gave him out of the world (v. 6). This revelation includes facts and a personal relationship with the Father (vv. 6–8). So when Jesus asks the Father to "protect them" (v. 11), he wants to safeguard the disciples' journey as they continue to know the Father and Son.

In Jesus's prayer: "Holy Father, protect them by the power of your name—the name you gave me" (v. 11), the *name* stands for God's character, revealed in Jesus.[18] He asks the Father himself to sustain believers. His words emphasize the Father's person with all of his love, power, and faithfulness. Believers are safe and sound in the Father's hands.

Prayer 2: That the Father Guard Believers as Jesus Did (v. 12)

Jesus asks the Father to protect believers in his absence just as Jesus did during his earthly ministry: "Holy Father, protect them. . . . While I was with them, I protected them" (vv. 11–12). As God the Son, Jesus gave eternal life to his eleven disciples and sustained them while he was with them. Verse eleven is Jesus's request for the Father to continue the work Jesus began on earth—preserving the disciples for final salvation. In this way John 17 resembles John 10. There we saw that the sheep are safe in the mighty arms of the Son and the Father. Here the Son says that he preserved his own while on earth and asks the Father to keep safeguarding them from heaven.

Jesus uses repetition to underscore his preservation of Christians: "I protected them and kept them safe. . . . None has been lost." (v. 12). Jesus adds keeping to protecting in order to underline his upholding the eleven persevering disciples. He has watched over them so they would not fall away.

Although some say that Jesus's words show that Judas lost his salvation, this is a mistake.[19] Jesus says, "None of them has been lost except the one doomed to destruction" (v. 12). Judas was one of Jesus's twelve disciples, but he was never a believer. There are at least four reasons for this conclusion. First, although Jesus chose Judas as a disciple, from the beginning Jesus knew that Judas would not believe and would betray him (John 6:64, 70–71).

Second, Judas opposes Mary, Lazarus's sister, when she anoints Jesus's feet with costly ointment. Judas protested that it should have been sold and the proceeds given to the poor (12:3–5, 7). John exposes Judas's motive: "He did not say this because he cared about the poor but because he was a thief; as keeper of the money bag, he used to help himself to what was put into it." (v. 6). Judas "*used to* help himself" indicates repeated or habitual action. Judas regularly stole the Lord's money! Warning against hypocrisy, Paul says that the unrighteous, including "thieves," will not inherit God's kingdom (1 Cor. 6:9). A Christian could steal, even as a Christian could commit idolatry or adultery. But persons living a lifestyle of stealing, idolatry, or adultery belie their profession to be Christians. Judas was a thief who had never been saved. His betrayal of Jesus was not an act that cut across the grain of his character. Rather, it revealed his character; it expressed his evil, unbelieving heart.

Third, as Jesus washed the disciples' feet, he said, "'Those who have had a bath need only to wash their feet; their whole body is clean. And you are clean, though not every one of you.' For he knew who was going to betray him, and that was why he said not everyone was clean" (John 13:10–11). The eleven disciples had "bathed" (been forgiven by God once and for all) and needed only to have their "feet washed" (to daily confess their sins). But Judas never knew the forgiveness of sins involved in conversion; he was not clean.

Fourth, both divine sovereignty and human responsibility point to the fact that Judas was not a believer. God is sovereign over all, even when his Son is betrayed. From the beginning Jesus knew who would betray him (6:64). Jesus predicted Judas's betrayal to prove that he is God (13:19). Jesus prayed, "While I was with them, I protected them and kept them safe by that name you gave me. None has been lost except the one doomed to destruction *so that Scripture would be fulfilled*" (17:12, emphasis added). The betrayal of Jesus fulfilled God's sovereign plan, as other Scriptures attest (Luke 22:22; Acts 2:23; 4:27–28). God was not surprised. Nevertheless, Judas is guilty and responsible for his actions. He regularly stole from the purse (John 12:6). Only he among the Twelve gave Satan an opening to exploit (13:2, 27). When Jesus identifies his betrayer, saying, "It is the one to whom I will give this piece of bread when I have dipped it in the dish" (v. 26), Judas freely takes the morsel from Jesus.

Schreiner and Caneday are correct:

> Jesus' very point in bringing up Judas is that he was an exception from the beginning. He was never . . . among those given by the Father to the Son. He was never washed and cleansed in the saving bath. It was prophesied from the outset that he would fulfill the role of betrayer. Thus, Jesus did not lose a single one of those given to him by God, and we are strengthened immeasurably when we realize that this prayer of Jesus will certainly be answered. God will keep us to the end and will unquestionably answer the prayers of his Son.[20]

Prayer 3: That the Father Shield Them from the Devil (v. 15)

Jesus continues praying for the disciples: "My prayer is not that you take them out of the world but that you protect them from the evil one" (v. 15). Again Jesus asks the Father to keep his own—and he unmasks the enemy—"from the evil one." In John's Gospel Jesus informs us about this evil one: "The devil . . . was a murderer from the beginning . . . he is a liar and the father of lies" (8:44). Jesus calls him "the prince of this world" and announces the enemy's rout (12:31; 14:30; 16:11). It is this devil, called Satan, who instigated Judas Iscariot to betray Jesus and empowered him for the foul deed (13:2, 27).

Jesus does not ask the Father to take the other eleven disciples out of this hostile world but to guard them from the evil one. Jesus knows that the devil is active and will entice his followers. If left to themselves, the Eleven would fall just like Judas. But because Jesus asked the Father to protect them from the devil, they are not left to themselves. The Son's prayers and the Father's power preserve them from evil. Because of the ministries of the Father and Son, even frightened Christians can take heart in John's words, "The one who is in you is greater than the one who is in the world" (1 John 4:4).

Prayer 4: That the Father Bring Believers to Heaven (v. 24)

Throughout this famous prayer, Jesus acts as if he has already returned to the Father in heaven. This is clearest in John 17:24: "Father, I want those you have given me to be with me where I am, and to see my glory, the glory you have given me." Jesus is on earth, preparing to go to the cross, yet he is certain of his victorious resurrection and ascension. He wants the Father to bring believers to join him in heaven so they can see his heavenly glory. Doubtless, the Father will delight to answer the prayer of his beloved Son. Believers will not fail to see Jesus's glory. In this way, Jesus ends his famous prayer with another confirmation of the preservation of God's people.

The harmony between the Father and the Son in salvation that we saw in John 10:28–30 also appears in John 17. As he opens his heart to his heavenly Father before his death and resurrection, Jesus emphasizes the fact that he protected his disciples spiritually while he was with them (except for Judas, who was never saved; see 17:12). Now, as Jesus prepares to return to the Father, Jesus asks him to continue to keep his chosen ones in Jesus's absence. Specifically, he asks the Father not to remove them from the hostile world but to protect them from Satan. Jesus ends his prayer by asking the Father to bring the chosen ones to heavenly glory.

ASSURANCE?

Ironically, believers in Christ can be assured by the sad story of Judas Iscariot. He was both a hypocrite and an apostate. He pretended to believe in Jesus, but for the reasons outlined above, he never truly did. He apostatized, abandoning a faith that he formerly professed. One of the reasons God includes hypocrites and apostates in his Word is to comfort Christians. How does this work? Graciously, God tells us ahead of time that some people will appear to be Christians but will not really be such (1 John 2:19). Some will defect from the people of God like Judas.

When professed Christians deny the faith like Dan Barker, whom we met in chapter 1 (pp. 27–28), we need not despair. Such defections do not undermine Scripture but prove it to be true, because it predicted that such things would happen. God told us in advance that there would be hypocrites so that when one is exposed, we would not lose faith. We should expect such things to occur. Of course, we don't want to witness hypocrisy or apostasy. But the Bible would not be true if such things never happened. They already began in the first century (as the antichrists and Judas attest). And, sadly, there will continue to be hypocrites and apostates until Jesus comes again to set wrongs right.

Jesus prays that the Father would protect his children's salvation in four different ways in John 17. How exciting that when Jesus prays to his Father on our behalf, he thinks of assuring us that we will not fail to enter his heavenly kingdom. How kind of him! That these proofs of our assurance appear during a heartfelt prayer of the Son to the Father should encourage our relationship with the Father and the Son. Clearly they are relational beings. And, astonishingly, they desire a relationship with us. Jesus prays that the Father would glorify Jesus in his death and resurrection so that God's people would enjoy eternal life. Then Jesus defines eternal life as knowing the Father and the Son (vv. 2–3). But we don't have to find out the hard way. We can submit to him without sowing the wild oats of rebellion, as some have done. Moreover, like Ruth Tucker, whom we met in chapter 1 (pp. 18–19), we can submit to the gracious Son of God, who loved us and gave himself for us, even when we have doubts.

CHAPTER 4

ASSURANCE AND PRESERVATION IN PAUL

Bill has a track record of persistent failure, both in academic studies and personal relationships. His family places considerable emphasis upon success and the achievement of status, and have made it clear that they regard him as something of a disappointment. He hasn't met the standards of his high-achieving parents. As a result, he has now acquired a deeply ingrained sense of failure and personal inability. Bill finds the gospel intimidating, because it seems to make demands which he feels he cannot meet. He is frightened of failing God. He has genuine and deep doubts and anxieties about whether he can ever really be a Christian.[1]

People like Bill suffer from the failure to meet high standards. The standards have various sources: some come from without, from parents or teachers, and some from within, where people are driven to excel for reasons they cannot always explain. Regardless of the source, consistent failure takes its toll, and as a result many feel inadequate and unworthy. Scripture has good news for Bill and those like him, for it turns our attention away from ourselves and our failures (and successes!)

and points us to Jesus in his death and resurrection. God's promises based on Jesus's saving work are mighty bulwarks of assurance. Even those beaten down by unmet expectations can gain a real measure of assurance by God's grace through faith in Christ.

In the previous chapter we saw five passages in John's writings that strengthen believers' assurance of salvation. Here we focus on five passages in Paul's letters that do the same:

- Romans 8:1–3
- Romans 8:28–39
- Ephesians 1:13–14; 4:30
- Philippians 1:4–6
- 1 Thessalonians 5:23–24

ROMANS 8:1-3

Therefore, there is now no condemnation for those who are in Christ Jesus, because through Christ Jesus the law of the Spirit who gives life has set you free from the law of sin and death. For what the law was powerless to do because it was weakened by the flesh, God did by sending his own Son in the likeness of sinful flesh to be a sin offering. And so he condemned sin in the flesh.[2]

Paul pens many passages to assure those who believe God's Word that they are saved and kept by God's sovereign grace. Romans 8 is the most famous and rightly so. From beginning to end this chapter provides Scripture's most substantial evidence of believers' safety in Christ and resultant assurance. Paul says, "Therefore, there is now no condemnation for those who are in Christ Jesus" (Rom. 8:1). The word *condemnation* occurs in the New Testament only in Romans 5:16, 18, and 8:1 and this suggests that in Romans 8:1–3, Paul draws conclusions from Romans 5:12–21. There he contrasted the two Adams and the consequences they brought to the people they each represent. Adam's sin in the garden of Eden brought condemnation and death to humanity. But Christ's "one act of righteousness" brought justification and eternal life to all who trust him for salvation (vv. 18–19).

No Condemnation

The background of the courtroom illuminates Paul's words: "Therefore, there is now no condemnation for those who are in Christ Jesus" (Rom. 8:1). Adopting legal language, the apostle asserts that Christ rescues his people from the penalty that all lawbreakers deserve—"condemnation." Jesus delivers believers from hell, the destiny of the condemned. The apostle is emphatic: "there is *no* condemnation" and never will be.[3] Jesus secured an eternal redemption for his people (cf. Heb. 9:12).

Paul joins legal with relational language when he proclaims that this salvation is for all "who are in Christ Jesus." All who died and rose with Christ (Rom. 6:1–11) are united to him spiritually and will be spared condemnation, "since the condemnation which they deserve has already been fully borne for them by Him,"[4] as verse 3 clarifies.

Liberated

"Because through Christ Jesus the law of the Spirit who gives life has set you free from the law of sin and death" (Rom. 8:2). The apostle provides the basis for verse 1: the Holy Spirit has freed believers from the Mosaic law's threat of condemnation for lawbreakers. As Paul notes, the Spirit is "the Spirit who gives life" because he quickens those who are spiritually dead. In this way the Spirit liberates us from the law that leads to sin and death. The life-giving Spirit transfers us from the kingdom of sin and death into the kingdom of righteousness and eternal life. Consequently, sin's penalty and power are defeated. Believers are delivered from condemnation (v. 1) and need not live under sin's cruel domination (vv. 4–17).

Sin Condemned

"For what the law was powerless to do because it was weakened by the flesh, God did by sending his own Son in the likeness of sinful flesh to be a sin offering. And so he condemned sin in the flesh" (Rom. 8:3). The law of Moses is "weakened by the flesh," that is, the law does not save because fallen people cannot keep it. But what the law was powerless to do, God did in Christ, whom he sent "in the likeness of sinful flesh."

Paul speaks carefully. He does not say, "Christ came in sinful flesh," for then he would be a sinner himself, unable to rescue others. Paul does not deny that Christ identified with sinners, for then too he could not rescue us because he could not represent us. Paul steers a middle course: Christ came "in the likeness of sinful flesh," genuinely sharing humanity with sinners while being sinless himself. In addition, the Father sent his Son "in the likeness of sinful flesh *to be a sin offering*." Paul refers to Christ's death as a sacrifice which takes away sin.[5]

So how did God, "by sending his own Son in the likeness of sinful flesh to be a sin offering," condemn sin in his Son's humanity? Douglas Moo answers well:

> The condemnation of sin consists in God's executing his judgment on sin in the atoning death of his Son. As our substitute, Christ "was made sin for us" (2 Cor. 5:21) and suffered the wrath of God, the judgment of God upon that sin. . . . In his doing so, of course, we may say that sin's power was broken in the sense that Paul pictures sin as a power that holds people in its clutches and brings condemnation to them. . . . The condemnation that our sins deserve has been poured out on Christ, our sin-bearer; that is why "there is now no condemnation for those who are in Christ Jesus" [Rom. 8:1].[6]

God sent his Son not only to liberate unsaved persons from condemnation (vv. 1–4a) but also to build godliness into their lives (vv. 4b–11). Christ died to justify *and* to progressively sanctify believers.

Summary

Paul opens Romans 8 with the declaration that God saves and keeps his people. He announces, "Therefore, there is now no condemnation for those who are in Christ Jesus" (Rom. 8:1).

Paul's words can be a healing balm for Christians stressed by the poor example of others. There certainly are hypocrites whose lives falsify their claims to know Christ and who harm his reputation in the world. There are also those who, after years of professing to believe the gospel, walk away from the faith, sometimes belligerently. These situations are difficult to observe and cause for lament. But they are not good reasons to question the truth of God's Word or the assurance of salvation it promises. Paul assures believers in Christ that there is no doom—no condemnation—for them. Hypocrites and apostates will have to answer to Christ for their lives. Their bad examples sometimes wound us, and by God's grace we continue to pray for them. But at the end of the day, we must leave them to the Lord. We don't withdraw from hypocrites and apostates. But we also don't base our lives on theirs. Instead, we base our lives on the Word of God and its promises. Among them are the grand words of assurance of Romans 8:1–3. The Father sent his Son to condemn sin in the flesh so we would not be condemned. That strengthens our faith regardless of what is going on around us. For that, we are grateful to him who loved us and gave himself for us (Gal. 2:20).

ROMANS 8:28-39

And we know that in all things God works for the good of those who love him, who have been called according to his purpose. For those God foreknew he also predestined to be conformed to the image of his Son, that he might be the firstborn among many brothers and sisters. And those he predestined, he also called; those he called, he also justified; those he justified, he also glorified. What, then, shall we say in response to these things? If God is for us, who can be against us? He who did not spare his own Son, but gave him up for us all—how will he not also, along with him, graciously give us all things? Who will bring any charge against those whom God has chosen? It is God who justifies. Who then is the one who condemns? No one. Christ Jesus who died—more than that, who was raised to life—is at the right hand of God and is also interceding for us. Who shall separate us from the love of Christ? Shall trouble or hardship or persecution or famine or nakedness or danger or sword? As it is written: "For your sake we face death all day long; we are considered as sheep to be slaughtered." No, in all these things we are more than conquerors through him who loved us. For I am convinced that neither death nor life, neither angels nor demons, neither the present nor the future, nor any powers, neither height nor depth, nor anything else in all creation, will be able to separate us from the love of God that is in Christ Jesus our Lord.

Paul's words in Romans 8:28–39 are the most compelling on the subject of preservation anywhere in Scripture. I say this for two reasons. First, their purpose is to teach preservation. Second, this is the most extensive biblical passage teaching that God keeps his saints.

Familiar words lead off: "And we know that in all things God works for the good of those who love him, who have been called according to his purpose" (Rom. 8:28). In context, "all things" means even "present sufferings" (v. 18). Those who love God, namely believers, should realize that God works all things, even their difficulties and pain, for their ultimate good. Paul tells us how: God has planned their greatest benefit, their final salvation (vv. 29–30). The apostle here begins the first of four arguments for why Christians are safe in God's grace. He bases each argument on one of God's qualities: God will preserve his saints because of his sovereignty (vv. 29–30), might (vv. 31–32), justice (vv. 33–34), and compassion (vv. 35–39).

We Are Safe Because of God's Sovereignty (vv. 29-30)

Paul begins verses 29–30 with the Greek word meaning *for* or *because* to explain how we know that God works all things for our ultimate benefit. It is because he has planned salvation, our highest good, from start to finish. Paul employs five verbs in the past tense to set forth God's plan. God is the subject of each verb, and God's people are the direct object of each verb. God foreknew, predestined, called, justified, and glorified believers.

God foreknew his saints. *Foreknow* and *foreknowledge* have several meanings in the New Testament. They refer to God's choosing Christ (Acts 2:23; 1 Peter 1:20) and to people knowing facts beforehand (Acts 26:5; 2 Peter 3:17). But whenever God is the one who foreknows and Christians are the ones he foreknows, *foreknew* and *foreknowledge* refer to God's prior love for them (Rom. 8:29; 11:2; 1 Peter 1:2).

For two reasons *foreknew* in Romans 8:29 does not mean that God knows facts beforehand, including who would believe in Christ. (Of course, God knows all facts, including these, but that is simply not what Romans 8:29 is talking about.) First, here God does not foreknow facts but people: "those God foreknew." Second, here only *some* are foreknown. Paul would say that all were foreknown if he meant that God knew people's responses to the gospel beforehand. But Paul says some, not all, are foreknown because the ones foreknown are the same people who are predestined, called, justified, and glorified. Plainly, not all human beings will be glorified. Therefore, in this text God foreknows some and not all people—that is, he loved them beforehand. Elsewhere Paul tells us how far beforehand—"before the foundation of the world" (Eph. 1:4 ESV) and "before the ages began" (2 Tim. 1:9 ESV).

Those he foreknew, God "also predestined" (v. 29). Predestination is God in sovereign mercy choosing people for salvation.[7] Paul writes succinctly, "God . . . has saved us and called us to a holy life—not because of anything we have done but because of *his own purpose and grace*. This grace was given us in Christ Jesus before the beginning of time" (2 Tim. 1:8–9). The apostle highlights predestination more than the other four verbs in Romans 8:29–30. Notice that it is only this verb that Paul expands: we were "predestined to be conformed to the image of his Son, that he might be the firstborn among many brothers and sisters" (v. 29). All who become God's children by faith in his Son (John 1:12; Gal. 3:24) will be conformed to his character. This is a great encouragement for us who frequently struggle with temptation!

Paul says, "And those he predestined, he also called" (Rom. 8:30). He means those God chose for salvation he successfully summons to Christ in the gospel. God "calls" them by bringing them to believe in his Son. "And those he called, he also justified." Those God summons to Christ, he declares righteous based on Christ's saving death and resurrection.

Paul's next words concern God's preservation of his people. He says, "Those he justified, he also glorified" (v. 30). Remarkably, glorification, a future aspect of salvation, appears in the past tense like the other four verbs. Glorification is the act of God's grace by which his resurrected people see Christ's glory and are thereby transformed so they share that glory (Col. 3:4; 2 Thess. 2:14; 1 Peter 5:1). Why does Paul put future glorification in the past tense? "Those he justified, he also *glorified.*" He does so to present all five actions in the same way, as accomplished realities. Thomas Schreiner explains, "What is envisioned is the eschatological completion of God's work on behalf of believers that began before history, and the aorist signifies the certainty that what God has begun he will finish."[8] We who know Christ and fight against sin now will one day fight no more. We will be glorified and in turn will glorify God for such a great salvation.

Almighty God keeps every one of his foreloved, predestined, called, and justified people for ultimate salvation—glorification. This is indicated by Paul's use of pronouns: "For *those* God foreknew he also predestined to be conformed to the image of his Son. . . . And *those* he predestined, he also called; *those* he called, he also justified; *those* he justified, he also glorified" (vv. 29–30). No one who trusts Christ for redemption will fail to be saved.

Our sovereign heavenly Father will keep every believer safe in his Son for final glorification.

We Are Safe Because of God's Might (vv. 31–32)

Paul bases his case for preservation on God's sovereignty and next on God's might. Paul is overcome by God's great grace: "What, then, shall we say in response to these things?" (Rom. 8:31). He then asks, "If God is for us, who can be against us?" (v. 31). By this rhetorical question Paul declares that absolutely nothing can defeat Christians if the almighty God is on their side. There is no question concerning his ability to protect his people. But how do we know God *will* do so? How can we be certain he is "for us" (v. 31)?

Paul replies to these questions with another rhetorical one: "He who did not spare his own Son, but gave him up for us all—how will he not also, along with him, graciously give us all things?" (v. 32). God sent his beloved Son to die in our place— that is the consummate proof of God's devoted love for us. If believers ever question whether God is on their side, they only need to remember Christ's cross. The cross shouts God's unqualified yes to all such questions! No foes can overpower the Creator of heaven and earth to remove us from his care. Our heavenly Father has pledged himself to us in the covenant, oath, and blood of his Son. He will never cast us out, but along with Jesus he will "graciously give us all things" (v. 32). Paul means that we, the sons and daughters of almighty God, will inherit the Trinity as well as the new heavens and new earth (Rom. 8:17; 1 Cor. 3:21–23)!

We Are Safe Because of God's Justice (vv. 33–34)

Paul argues for our preservation in Christ because of God's sovereignty, might, and justice. Once more he leads with a rhetorical question: "Who will bring any charge against those whom God has chosen?" (Rom. 8:33). His words signify that "no one will make a legal accusation against Christians that holds up in

God's court." He does not mince words: "It is God who justifies" (v. 33). Our appeal has gone all the way to the heavenly supreme court, and the supreme Judge has declared us not guilty. We deserved God the Father's verdict of "guilty" because of our sins, but seeing us in Christ, he has rendered a verdict of "righteous." This verdict of God, the highest Judge, will never be reversed. So, once again, Paul argues that we are safe because of who God is—just—and what he has done for us—justified us in Christ.

Then, slightly varying his language, Paul makes a similar argument. Again he begins with a rhetorical question: "Who then is the one who condemns" (v. 34)? Biblically speaking, the judge presiding over the last judgment varies: sometimes it is the Father and sometimes the Son. When the apostle, therefore, names "Christ Jesus" after he asks who will condemn, it is natural to think that he is preparing us to see Christ as judge. But that isn't the case. Rather, Paul says, "Christ Jesus who died—more than that, who was raised to life—is at the right hand of God and is also interceding for us" (v. 34). Christ, along with the Father, the judge of all, will not condemn believers at the last judgment. Why? Christ is not acting as our judge but as our redeemer. He laid down his life, was resurrected, ascended to God's right hand, and intercedes for us when the devil accuses us before God's throne. Believers will meet Jesus the judge as their savior!

At present Jesus intercedes before God for us to keep us saved. His intercession involves both the presence of his sacrifice in heaven (Heb. 7:23–25) as well as his pleas for us (Rom. 8:34). Paul has prayer in mind here. In the preceding verses, Paul twice speaks of the Holy Spirit's intercession by offering prayers on our behalf: "In the same way, the Spirit helps us in our weakness. We do not know what we ought to pray for, but the Spirit himself intercedes for us through wordless groans. And he who searches our hearts knows the mind of the Spirit, because the Spirit intercedes for God's people in accordance with the will of God" (vv. 26–27).

Christ the judge, who will condemn sinners, will not condemn his people, whom he rescues and preserves by his intercession.

God's justice assures us of final salvation because of the Father's legal decision and the Son's prayers. Schreiner is right: "God being for believers means that no legal charge will be leveled against them on the eschatological day" (vv. 33–34).[9]

We Are Safe Because of God's Compassion (vv. 35-39)

Paul saves the best for last—his argument for believers' safety in Christ based on his compassion. He begins yet again with rhetorical questions: "Who shall separate us from the love of Christ? Shall trouble or hardship or persecution or famine or nakedness or danger or sword?" (Rom. 8:35). He lists seven foes to ponder what could possibly remove Christians from their Savior's grace.[10] The first six enemies comprise severe problems terminating in death ("sword"). Paul cites Psalm 44:22 to convince the Romans that their difficulties, even harsh ones, are not uncommon. The Old Testament saints were acquainted with suffering too: "As it is written: 'For your sake we face death all day long; we are considered as sheep to be slaughtered'" (v. 36).

Paul has built tension by first pondering what could possibly take away Christians from Jesus's love. Then he replies negatively: "No, in all these things we are more than conquerors through him who loved us" (v. 37). Believers will not be torn apart from the one to whom they were joined in salvation. Instead, they will remain in union with him and triumph through his love. Paul is emphatic: we are more than conquerors—we overwhelmingly triumph—through our redeemer's compassion.

Paul's case for divine protection reaches its climax when he forsakes rhetorical questions for all-embracing assertions: "For I am convinced that neither death nor life, neither angels nor demons, neither the present nor the future, nor any powers, neither height nor depth, nor anything else in all creation, will be able to separate us from the love of God that is in Christ Jesus our Lord" (vv. 38–39). Except for the term *powers*, Paul uses pairs of items to emphasize his point—absolutely nothing at all will ever take God's people away from Jesus's mercy.

"Neither death nor life" will separate them. *Life* and *death* totally sum up our experience. Here *angels* and *demons* refer to evil angels, who want to destroy Christians. The recipients of Paul's letter to the Romans considered them as a real menace, even though few of us take them seriously today. Paul insists that evil angels will fail to separate God's people from their Savior. Again Paul speaks exhaustively, now with reference to time: "neither the present nor the future." Nothing present or future will ever sever us from Christ's compassion.

Paul writes *powers* to denote demons, who despite their designation are powerless to take believers away from their Savior. *Height* and *depth* refer to space: nothing "above" or "below," not heaven or hell, will separate us from Christ. Again the apostle ranges far and wide: "nor anything else in all creation, will be able to separate us from the love of God that is in Christ Jesus our Lord" (v. 39). The Creator and his creatures are everything that exists. Again and again, God through his apostle has announced his purpose to sustain his people for final salvation. Now he adds "nor anything else in all creation" will doom us. Paul's language is intense. We are safe in the Savior's compassion, and God will never allow anything to divorce us from it.

There is much help here for believers who doubt their salvation. Ruth Tucker (pp. 18–19) keeps coming back to passages like this one when she insists that, despite her self-doubting, God will not let her go. Although Ruth does not always feel saved, a product of the separation of head and heart in her formative church experience, she knows God's promise of salvation is rock-solid. This enables her to lay her head on her pillow at night and to sleep in peace. Her salvation does not depend on her grip on God; it depends on his secure embrace of her.

EPHESIANS 1:13–14; 4:30

And you also were included in Christ when you heard the
message of truth, the gospel of your salvation. When you

believed, you were marked in him with a seal, the promised Holy Spirit, who is a deposit guaranteeing our inheritance until the redemption of those who are God's possession—to the praise of his glory. (1:13–14)

And do not grieve the Holy Spirit of God, with whom you were sealed for the day of redemption. (4:30)

Up until now we have examined preservation passages that put the spotlight on the Father's seal and pledge of our ultimate deliverance.[11] Here Paul writes in Trinitarian terms. He draws attention to the roles played by the three persons of the Trinity in salvation. The apostle praises the Father for choosing sinners for salvation (vv. 4–5, 11). He exalts the Son for redeeming us "through his blood" (v. 7). And he extols the Holy Spirit (v. 13).

The Spirit Plays a Role in Salvation

Paul speaks of the role that the Spirit plays in salvation: "In him you also, when you heard the word of truth, the gospel of your salvation, and believed in him, were sealed with the promised Holy Spirit" (v. 13 ESV). When the Ephesians trusted Christ as Lord and Savior, God sealed them. Paul employs a divine passive—"you were sealed"—to draw attention to the Father as one who seals. In another passage Paul indicates that the Father seals Christians with the Spirit. He does this by distinguishing God (2 Cor. 1:21) from Christ (v. 21) and the Spirit (v. 22).

The seal is the Holy Spirit, as prophesied by the Old Testament. Simplifying Paul's language in Ephesians 1:13 helps get the point across: "In him you . . . were sealed with the promised Holy Spirit" (v. 13 ESV). Believers in Christ were sealed "in him," that is, in Christ. And they were sealed with the Spirit. All three persons of the Trinity, then, are involved in our sealing. The Father seals believers with the seal of the Spirit in union with Christ. God seals our spiritual union with Christ by giving us the Spirit. This is one way of teaching that our union with Christ is made secure.

The Father joins us to his Son to give us all of his saving benefits. He sends the Spirit into our hearts as his seal, pledging that he will keep us saved.

Old and New Testaments show people sealing things to indicate ownership or authentication and security. Pharaoh gave Joseph his signet ring to signify authentication (Gen. 41:42). When Joseph seals a document with pharaoh's ring, it certifies that the message carries pharaoh's authority. In the New Testament Paul tells the Corinthian congregation they are "the seal of" his "apostleship in the Lord" (1 Cor. 9:2). Their existence as a Christian church authenticates his apostleship.

Seals also provide security or protection. After the stone was placed over the mouth of the lions' den, closing Daniel inside, King Darius sealed the stone with his ring to make it secure (Dan. 6:17). The same is true of the tomb into which Jesus's crucified body was laid. The soldiers "made the tomb secure by putting a seal on the stone and posting the guard" (Matt. 27:66). John combines the two uses in Revelation 7:2–8 and 9:4 when God seals the 144,000 believers. The seal marks them as God's people and shields them from the angel of death.

The Spirit Is God's Seal

As God's seal, the Holy Spirit likewise indicates ownership and security. He marks believers as God's people: "Now it is God who makes both us and you stand firm in Christ. He anointed us, *set his seal of ownership on us*, and put his Spirit in our hearts as a deposit, guaranteeing what is to come" (2 Cor. 1:21–22). Three times Paul refers to the Spirit here. He is God's anointing, seal, and deposit. Seal indicates ownership and deposit indicates security as the words following the word *deposit* indicate: "guaranteeing what is to come."

Being sealed with the Spirit expresses safety in Christ. Paul brings this out in Ephesians when he explains that the Holy Spirit, with whom we are sealed, "is a deposit, guaranteeing our inheritance until the redemption of those who are God's possession—to the praise of his glory" (Eph. 1:13–14). The word *guarantee* is a business term denoting a deposit or down payment. God grants the Spirit now as a down payment on our future inheritance. That means our inheritance is safe because God gave us the Spirit to assure us of better things in the future.

Christians Are Safe

Paul spells out that the Spirit guarantees our final salvation: "And do not grieve the Holy Spirit of God, with whom you were sealed for the day of redemption" (Eph. 4:30). What sins of believers especially make the Spirit sad? The context points to sinful anger and speaking against others (vv. 26, 29, 31). Only once in Scripture do we read the full name of the Spirit: "the Holy Spirit of God" and that is here. Peter T. O'Brien remarks that this name "emphatically underscores the identity of the one who may be offended, and thus the seriousness of causing him distress."[12]

Once more Paul uses the passive voice, "you were sealed," to identify the Father as divine sealer. Paul declares God's goal of sealing when he says concerning the Spirit, "with whom you were sealed for the day of redemption." The Father sealed us in order to redeem us on the last day. Salvation is secure because it is guaranteed by the Spirit whom God sends to protect us "for the day of redemption."

Summary

In Ephesians 1:13–14 the three persons of the Trinity work together to keep God's people saved. The Father is the sealer. He seals Christians' union with Christ who died and arose to save them. The seal is the Holy Spirit. The three Trinitarian persons cooperate to secure the permanence of our salvation. Paul underlines his message by adding the picture of the Spirit as guarantee. When we believe the gospel we receive the Holy Spirit as God's promise of our final liberation. Paul clarifies by adding the goal of God's sealing: believers "were sealed *for the day of redemption*" (Eph. 4:30). Sealing, then, highlights God's keeping his people saved until the end. Judith Gundry Volf agrees: "Those who have been sealed with the Spirit thus come under divine protection until the end, when God will fully redeem God's own possession."[13]

PHILIPPIANS 1:4–6

In all my prayers for all of you, I always pray with joy because of your partnership in the gospel from the first day until now, being confident of this, that he who began a good work in you will carry it on to completion until the day of Christ Jesus.

Paul greets the Philippian congregation and its leaders, and then says that, whenever he thinks of them, he joyously thanks God on account of their "partnership in the gospel," from beginning to end.

God Will Continue

Paul wastes no time expressing his persuasion. He is "confident of this, that he who began a good work in you will carry it on to completion until the day of Christ Jesus" (v. 6). When Paul says, he is "confident of this," he expresses trust in God. He is convinced that God will continue his work in his saints in Philippi. Paul expresses his conviction at a beginning point and an end point. First, he speaks of God's beginning "a good work" in the Philippians. Paul alludes to their reception of the gospel (as told in Acts 16:11–40). Then Paul speaks of an end point—"the day of Christ Jesus," which is a reference to Christ's return.

A Very Good Work

What is "the good work" God began in the Philippians that he will sustain until the second coming? To answer that, we need some background information from Genesis and Isaiah. Genesis 1–2 tells of God's original "good work" of creation. Isaiah uses creation language from Genesis to speak of God's "work" of the new creation.

Paul touches on the new creation, one of his favorite topics. Following Isaiah's lead, the apostle employs the language of Genesis 1–2 to tell of the new age of salvation launched by Christ's death and resurrection. In the drama of the new creation Christ plays the role of "the last Adam," "the second man" (1 Cor. 15:45, 47). The new age will only be fully manifested in the new heavens and the new earth, but it was already inaugurated in Jesus's resurrection (1 Cor. 15:20; Col. 1:18).

Genesis 2:2 reports God's primal good work: "By the seventh day God had finished the work he had been doing; so on the seventh day he rested from all his work." Paul tells of another "good work" that God will complete: "that *work* of grace in the readers' lives that began with their reception of the gospel," as Peter T. O'Brien notes.[14] Isaiah employs creation language to tell of God summoning Israel to belong to him and of his redeeming and keeping them:

> This is what God the Lord says—
> the Creator of the heavens, who stretches them out,
>> who spreads out the earth with all that springs
>>> from it,
>> who gives breath to its people,
>> and life to those who walk on it:
> "I, the Lord, have called you in righteousness;
>> I will take hold of your hand.
> I will keep you and will make you
>> to be a covenant for the people
>> and a light for the Gentiles." (Isa. 42:5–6)

> But now, this is what the Lord says—
>> he who created you, Jacob,
>> he who formed you, Israel:
> "Do not fear, for I have redeemed you;
>> I have summoned you by name; you are mine."
>> (43:1)

Until Jesus Returns

When Paul speaks of "a good work" that God began among the Philippians, he refers to his powerful work of redemption in their midst. Viewed against Old Testament precedents in Genesis and Isaiah, Philippians 1:6 heralds the fact that the Creator of the heavens and the earth, God Almighty himself, who delivered Old Testament Israel, will complete the saving work he began in the Philippian church. Indeed, Paul's attention to the end of history "draws attention to the faithfulness of God in completing that good work on the day of Christ, a reference to the second coming or parousia of the Lord."[15]

Paul speaks again of God's work among the Philippians: "For it is God who works in you to will and to act in order to fulfill his good purpose" (Phil. 2:13). Because this is true, Paul begins his letter with assurance that "he who began a good work in you will carry it on to completion until the day of Christ Jesus" (Phil. 1:6). Paul starts his letter declaring that God, who began a work of new creation in them when they trusted Christ, will maintain that work until Jesus returns.

1 THESSALONIANS 5:23-24

> May God himself, the God of peace, sanctify you through and through. May your whole spirit, soul and body be kept blameless at the coming of our Lord Jesus Christ. The one who calls you is faithful, and he will do it.

Paul includes a wish-prayer near the end of 1 Thessalonians. A wish-prayer is both an expression of good will (a wish) and a prayer that God would grant the wish.[16] Paul asks God to bring about his hearers' sanctification, which he had prayed for earlier (3:11–13; 4:3–6). He asks God to consecrate the Thessalonians through and through. He realizes that, although believers have a part in their growth in holiness, only God can bring it to completion. Therefore, he begins his prayer: "May God *himself*, the God of peace . . ."

This final sanctification is so significant to Paul that he repeats himself. He prays another wish prayer that the Thessalonians would be kept blamelessly until Christ returns. He enlarges the concept of their being completely sanctified when he prays that their "whole spirit, soul and body be kept blameless at the coming of our Lord Jesus Christ." "Your whole spirit, soul and body" is an expansion of "through and through." Paul is accentuating his point.

Thus twice at the end of his epistle Paul asks God to bring about the perfect sanctification of the Thessalonians at the second coming. Verse 24 is vital to our investigation of preservation and assurance. Fee is correct: "It is of high interest that Paul concludes his prayer for them with an affirmation regarding its being realized. It has to do not so much with their effort—although he surely expects them to do their part—as with God's own faithfulness."[17] Paul not only prays for his readers' complete consecration; he expects God to do it, citing God's faithfulness as his confidence: "The one who calls you is faithful, and he will do it" (v. 24). As surely as God is faithful, he will finally and completely sanctify the Thessalonian believers.

Summary

No one describes 1 Thessalonians 5:24 better than Leon Morris:

> Paul's prayer is no despairing wail, but a cry of faith. He is supremely confident that what he has asked will be done, and this verse reveals that the ground of his trust is in the nature of God. . . . Now we see that he is sure that God will indeed supply their need in this matter, because He is "faithful." . . . It is not in the unstable qualities of men that trust must be placed, but in the eternal faithfulness of God. . . .
>
> But God, besides being a Caller, is a Doer. . . . The God to whom Paul prays is not a God who is inactive or ineffective. Paul thinks of Him as One who will certainly bring to

completion that which he has begun. "Hath he said, and will he not do it?" (Num. 23:19). Because He is the faithful One, and because He is the One who has called them, they may know that He will do perfectly all that is involved in their call. It is profoundly satisfying to the believer that in the last resort what matters is not his feeble hold on God, but God's strong grip on him.[18]

WHAT DIFFERENCE DOES IT MAKE?

This chapter on Paul, like the previous one on John, has majored on God's promises to keep his own, the principal source of assurance. Paul confidently declares: "Therefore, there is now no condemnation for those who are in Christ Jesus" (Rom. 8:1). He then defends his declaration: Christ delivered us from the law's threat of judgment and God condemned sin through Christ's death. The apostle's longest passage on eternal security (vv. 28–39) argues on the basis of four divine attributes—God's sovereignty, might, justice, and compassion. God's sovereignty assures his plan's fulfillment, including our glorification. His might is supreme; we will triumph because the Father fulfills his pledge to us by sending his Son to die for us. He, the ultimate Judge, has pronounced us righteous in Christ, and that judgment will never be reversed. Moreover, nothing will ever separate the people who belong to God from his compassion.

Paul further assures us when he teaches that the Father has sealed our union with Christ by giving us the Holy Spirit as a seal "for the day of redemption" (Eph. 1:13–14; 4:30). God who "began a good work" of the new creation (salvation) in the Philippian congregation "will carry it on to completion until the day of Christ Jesus" (Phil. 1:6). Twice Paul prays for the entire sanctification of the Thessalonians, and then he declares: "The one who calls you is faithful, and he will do it" (1 Thess. 5:24). Paul provides abundant evidence of the fact that God will keep us saved and not let us go. This powerfully impacts our lives.

I once had a brilliant student, whom I will call Tom, who felt inferior to his fellow students because he claimed he "lacked the proper feelings of a Christian man." He was a sincere Christian who in his own estimation could not feel or express strong emotions in comparison to his more emotive friends. He was an outstanding scholar, and the papers he wrote in seminary were top-notch. But he tortured himself because, try as he might, he could not match the feelings that he observed in others. When asked if he believed the gospel, he professed Christ and beautifully explained his saving work. Moreover, his life backed up his profession. Importantly, his wife did not doubt his salvation but confirmed that he was a solid Christian, who wrongly punished himself because of his inability to feel.

Paradoxically, Tom's solution is identical to the one for people who put too much stock in their ability to feel God, who trust their emotions too much—think of Steve from chapter 1 (pp. 22–23). Steve and Tom need to stand on the promises of God, regardless of their feelings or lack thereof. God made us all different and some feel more deeply than others, just as some think more deeply than others. That is why the Lord graciously assures us in three ways: through the gospel, by his Spirit, and by working in our lives. He grants assurance through head, heart, and life. Those with "too much" or "too little" emotive ability must not let heart overwhelm head. They need to hold fast to the gospel and not put too much confidence in their ability or lack of ability to feel salvation.

PART 2

ASSURANCE
AND THE
HOLY SPIRIT

CHAPTER 5

THE HOLY SPIRIT'S PERSON AND WORK

God is a very good Father to his children! He not only sends his Son to save us from our sins but wants us to enjoy assurance of salvation. The Father shows his goodness by assuring us in three main ways. First and foremost, he assures us in his Word, making promises of salvation and preservation. The last three chapters studied those promises. God also assures us by working in our lives. That is the subject of chapter 7. This chapter and the next focus on a third way God comforts his people—the inner witness of the Holy Spirit.

Before we examine passages telling of the Spirit's inner witness in the next chapter, let's learn more about who the Holy Spirit is and what he does.

THE PERSON OF THE HOLY SPIRIT

The Spirit Is a Person

The Holy Spirit is a person, not an impersonal force.[1] The Spirit is a *he*, not an *it*. He has personal qualities and does things only persons do.

The Spirit can be known. Jesus predicts that, unlike the world, the disciples will know the Spirit: "And I will ask the Father, and he will give you another advocate to help you and be with you forever—the Spirit of truth. The world cannot accept him, because it neither sees him nor knows him. But you know him, for he lives with you and will be in you" (John 14:16–17). The world cannot receive the Spirit for it does not believe what it cannot see. Although Christians do not see the Spirit, the Spirit will dwell with and in them, and they will know him. Impersonal forces cannot be known in this way; only persons can. Since the Spirit can be known relationally, he is a person.

The Spirit thinks and communicates. Forces cannot think, but persons can. The Spirit thinks, for Paul speaks of "the mind of the Spirit" (Rom. 8:27). Paul shows the Spirit's mind: "The Spirit searches all things, even the deep things of God. For who knows a person's thoughts except their own spirit within them? In the same way no one knows the thoughts of God except the Spirit of God" (1 Cor. 2:10–11). The Spirit searches the depths of God and comprehends God's thoughts as only a person could.

The apostle shows that the Spirit communicates. The Spirit prays: "The Spirit intercedes for the saints in accordance with God's will" (Rom. 8:27). And he warns: "The Spirit clearly says that in later times some will abandon the faith and follow deceiving spirits and things taught by demons" (1 Tim. 4:1). Impersonal forces do not pray or warn. The Holy Spirit does both.

The Spirit wills and feels. Paul writes concerning spiritual gifts: "All these are the work of one and the same Spirit, and he distributes them to each one, just as he determines" (1 Cor. 12:11). The Spirit exercises his will in distributing gifts, something only persons do. Moreover, forces cannot be hurt. But Scripture implies that the Spirit can be hurt. Paul commands: "And do not grieve the Holy Spirit of God, with whom you were sealed for the day of redemption" (Eph. 4:30).

The Spirit helps and saves. Imprisoned, Paul looks to the Spirit for help: "for I know that through your prayers and God's provision of the Spirit of Jesus Christ what has happened to me will turn out for my deliverance" (Phil. 1:19). Unlike impersonal forces, the Spirit engages in rescue operations. He gives life: "The letter kills, but the Spirit gives life" (2 Cor. 3:6). He sanctifies: "God chose you as firstfruits to be saved through the sanctifying work of the Spirit and through belief in the truth" (2 Thess. 2:13). Only persons can give life and sanctify.

The Spirit Is God

The Spirit has divine attributes. Jesus calls the Spirit "the Spirit of truth" (John 14:17; 15:26; 16:13) because the Spirit performs the divine work of revealing Jesus, the truth (15:26; 16:13–15). The knowledge revealed by the Spirit of truth is divine knowledge, known only to the Trinity: the Spirit "will glorify me because it is from me that he will receive what he will make known to you. All that belongs to the Father is mine. That is why I said the Spirit will receive from me what he will make known to you" (16:14–15).

Overfamiliarity with the name *Holy Spirit* (14:26) has weakened its power. That is unfortunate, for the name links the Spirit with God's holiness in a way only appropriate to God himself. Thus truth and holiness are bound up with the Spirit's names and show him to be God.

The Spirit indwells believers. Only God indwells believers. A few times God the Son is said to indwell them (Gal. 2:20; Eph. 3:17; Col. 1:27). Usually, however, the Holy Spirit is the one indwelling believers (John 14:16–17; Rom. 8:9, 11; 1 Cor. 3:16; 2 Cor. 1:22). Since God alone indwells his people, the Spirit's indwelling reveals his divinity.

The Spirit is linked to the Father and the Son. Paul's most famous benediction reads: "May the grace of the Lord Jesus Christ, and the love of God, and the fellowship of the Holy Spirit be with you all" (2 Cor. 13:14). This reveals not only that the Holy Spirit is a person rather than a force—human beings cannot have "fellowship" with a force—but it also demonstrates the Spirit's deity, for the Spirit's divine blessing appears alongside the Son's and the Father's.

The Spirit applies salvation. The most significant evidence of the Spirit's deity is his role in salvation. The Spirit applies adoption by enabling believers to call God "Father" in truth: "The Spirit you received does not make you slaves, so that you live in fear again; rather, the Spirit you received brought about your adoption to sonship. And by him we cry, '*Abba*, Father'" (Rom. 8:15). The Spirit also applies justification to believers: "But you were washed, you were sanctified, you were justified in the name of the Lord Jesus Christ and by the Spirit of our God" (1 Cor. 6:11). The Spirit, along with the Father, will also play a role in our resurrection from the dead: "And if the Spirit of him who raised Jesus from the dead is living in you, he who raised Christ from the dead will also give life to your mortal bodies because of his Spirit who lives in you" (Rom. 8:11). Adoption, justification, and resurrection are each a different way of describing salvation. Because the Spirit plays a role in all three, the Spirit is God.

The Spirit plays a key role in redemption. He applies redemption to God's people. In fact, Scripture teaches that the Spirit is absolutely essential to salvation: "And if anyone does not have the Spirit of Christ, they do not belong to Christ" (Rom. 8:9).

THE WORKS OF THE HOLY SPIRIT

The Spirit performs many wonderful works.[2] He took part in creation and inspired Scripture. He is shown to work in the world, the apostles, and Jesus. One of his most important works for believers is his work in salvation: he joins people to Christ.

The Work of the Spirit in Creation

A few times Scripture mentions the Holy Spirit in relation to creation. The Bible begins: "In the beginning God created the heavens and the earth. Now the earth was formless and empty, darkness was over the surface of the deep, and the Spirit of God was hovering over the waters" (Gen. 1:1–2). I take "the Spirit of God was hovering over the waters" (v. 2) as a reference to the Holy Spirit participating in the divine activity of creation. Likewise, Elihu's words presuppose the Spirit's part in creation:

"The Spirit of God has made me; the breath of the Almighty gives me life" (Job 33:4).

The Work of the Spirit in Scripture

The Holy Spirit was involved in the production of Holy Scripture. Peter, discussing the Old Testament prophets, affirms: "Above all, you must understand that no prophecy of Scripture came about by the prophet's own interpretation of things. For prophecy never had its origin in the human will, but prophets, though human, spoke from God as they were carried along by the Holy Spirit" (2 Peter 1:20–21). Peter says that prophecies were not the product of mere human impulse but instead the prophets were impelled by the Holy Spirit so that they spoke from God himself.

The Work of the Spirit in the World

The Spirit also plays vital roles in the world. Jesus tells the disciples that it is good for him to leave because he will then send the Helper. What will the Helper do?

> When he comes, he will prove the world to be in the wrong about sin and righteousness and judgment: about sin, because people do not believe in me; about righteousness, because I am going to the Father, where you can see me no longer; and about judgment, because the prince of this world now stands condemned. (John 16:8–11)

How merciful Jesus is! He will send the Spirit to convict sinners of their sin "because people do not believe in" him (v. 9). On their own, sinners would not believe, but the Spirit convicts the world and points it toward Christ.

Furthermore, the Spirit is included in the chorus of witnesses to Jesus. In the Gospel of John, Jesus declares: "When the Advocate comes, whom I will send to you from the Father—the Spirit of truth who goes out from the Father—he will testify about me" (15:26). The Spirit thus joins John the Baptist, Jesus's miracles, the Old Testament, the Father, the disciples, and Jesus himself in witnessing to Jesus.

The Holy Spirit invites people to come to Christ. In some of the Bible's final words we read: "The Spirit and the bride say, 'Come!' And let the one who hears say, 'Come!' Let the one who is thirsty come; and let the one who wishes take the free gift of the water of life" (Rev. 22:17). God graciously ends his story with both the Spirit and the church warmly inviting readers to come to Jesus to quench their spiritual thirst.

The Work of the Spirit in the Apostles

The Spirit is active in the apostles and their ministries. He equips them to serve God. He teaches them what to say (Luke 12:12; 21:15) and empowers them at Pentecost to be witnesses to Jesus's sufferings and resurrection (24:48). The Spirit leads the apostles into the work he has prepared for them (Acts 13:2, 4). He guides their corporate judgments for the church (15:28). He shuts and opens doors of ministry so they preach the Word where God calls them (16:6–10).

Through the apostles' ministry, the Spirit builds the church as a holy temple to the Lord. Remarkably, God incorporates gentiles, who are foreigners to God and his covenants, into his people (Eph. 2:19–22). The church's foundation rests on Christ, its cornerstone, and his apostles and New Testament prophets. The Holy Spirit builds this structure, the church, by adding believing Jews and gentiles to God's people.

The Spirit also intercedes for the apostles and for all Christians. In ourselves we are weak and need the Lord's strength. Sometimes we do not even know how to pray. Thankfully, the Spirit prays to the Father in our behalf (Rom. 8:26–27).

The Work of the Spirit in Jesus

Remarkably, the same Spirit at work in the earthly ministry of Jesus works in the people of God. The Spirit was active in Old Testament predictions and Jesus's conception, earthly ministry, death, resurrection, and baptizing the church.

Isaiah foretells that the Coming One will be a descendant of King David. God's Spirit will rest on this "Branch" growing "from the stump of Jesse," granting him great wisdom and strength (11:1–3). The Lord will choose him to be his servant and will delight in him. The Lord will give him the Spirit, and the Coming One will act in justice, gentleness, and perseverance (42:1–4). The anointing of the Lord's Spirit will enable him to preach good news to the poor, the brokenhearted, the captives, and the imprisoned. He will bring comfort to some and vengeance to others (61:1–2). In these prophecies, the Holy Spirit prepared Israel for their Messiah.

According to the Scriptures, the Spirit is at work in the life of Jesus from the very beginning.[3] His conception in Mary's womb is the work of the Spirit. As the Holy Spirit came upon people in the Old Testament, so he comes upon Mary (Luke 1:35). From Jesus's conception, the Spirit of glory overwhelms Mary, and as a result, her baby boy is born "the holy one . . . the Son of God" (v. 35). In Mary's womb, the Spirit helps prepare a human body and soul for Jesus, so that he could save his people from their sins.

The Spirit is active in all aspects of Jesus's earthly ministry. At Jesus's baptism, the Spirit descends "on him like a dove," so that he can fulfill his threefold messianic office of prophet, priest, and king (Mark 1:10). "At once" the same Spirit drives "him out into the desert," where he is tempted by Satan for forty days (v. 12–13).

Jesus quotes Isaiah 61:1–2 in his first sermon: "The Spirit of the Lord is on me" (Luke 4:18). The Spirit *is* on Jesus and anoints him as prophet, priest, and king. Consequently, his earthly ministry is empowered by the Spirit (vv. 14–15). In contradiction to the Pharisees' blasphemous claims that Jesus casts out demons by the devil, he does so by the Spirit of God (Matt. 12:28). In fact, the Father gives the Son "the Spirit without limit" (John 3:34).

The Spirit also plays a role in Jesus's crucifixion. The writer to the Hebrews declares: "How much more, then, will the blood of Christ, who through the eternal Spirit offered himself unblemished to God, cleanse our consciences from acts that lead to death, so that we may serve the living God!" (Heb. 9:14). The Spirit is active in and through Jesus's atoning death. William Lane explains: the writer "indicates what makes Christ's sacrifice absolute and final. . . . The fact that his offering was made . . . 'through the eternal Spirit' implies that he has been divinely empowered and sustained in his office."[4]

Both Peter and Paul testify to the Spirit's activity in Jesus's resurrection. Peter writes, "For Christ also suffered once for sins, the righteous for the unrighteous, to bring you to God. He was put to death in the body but made alive in the Spirit" (1 Peter 3:18).[5] Paul agrees: Jesus "through the Spirit of holiness was appointed the Son of God in power by his resurrection from the dead: Jesus Christ our Lord" (Rom. 1:4). The Father appoints his Son in a new way by powerfully raising him from the dead through the agency of the Spirit.[6].

As the Christ, the Messiah, the Anointed One, Jesus is anointed by the Spirit at his baptism, and in response, he gives the Spirit. He does so when he baptizes the church with the Spirit at Pentecost in Acts 2 in fulfillment of prophecies (Joel 2:28; Luke 3:16; 24:49; Acts 1:4–5). We must understand that *Jesus* pours out the Spirit on the church at Pentecost. At Pentecost the Old Testament promises of a new covenant (Jer. 31:31) are fulfilled in him, the "one mediator between God and mankind" (1 Tim. 2:5). He is the mediator of the new covenant (Heb. 9:15), ratified by his death and resurrection (Luke 22:20), and this is proclaimed at Pentecost.

Although the new creation will only be fully disclosed at the end, Christ inaugurates the new creation when he dies, rises, and publicly proclaims the new creation at Pentecost. After his resurrection Jesus tells his disciples that he sends them as the Father sent him (John 20:21). He then performs a prophetic action to equip them for their mission: "And with that he breathed on them and said, 'Receive the Holy Spirit. If you forgive anyone's sins, their sins are forgiven; if you do not forgive them, they are not forgiven'" (John 20:22–23). Jesus breathes on the disciples much like God breathed life into Adam (Gen. 2:7). As the Creator granted life to his creature through the divine act of in-breathing, so also the risen Christ, the re-creator, by his prophetic act promises to give spiritual life to his disciples. Christ's breathing on them while saying "Receive the Holy Spirit" foreshadows the new creation that Pentecost will initiate, and that new creation begins with a new community in the church.

Jesus on the day of Pentecost gives the Holy Spirit to the people of God in a new and powerful manner. The Spirit brings the fullness of salvation. And that salvation manifests itself in many ways, including as an unprecedented witness. Christ forms a new community, the New Testament church, when he gives the Spirit at Pentecost.

The Main Work of the Spirit in Believers

Although the Holy Spirit performs many amazing works for believers, his chief work is uniting them to Christ. The Spirit unites us to the Son of God so that he and his saving benefits become ours. Paul teaches this in two ways. First, he directly ascribes our union with Christ to the Spirit. The Spirit is the bond of union. Second, the apostle ascribes to the Spirit's work aspects of salvation that occur in union with Christ. These include regeneration, justification, adoption, sanctification, and glorification.

The Spirit is the bond of union with Christ. Paul teaches that the Holy Spirit is essential to spiritual union: "Just as a body, though one, has many parts, but all its many parts form one body, so it is with Christ. For we were all baptized by one Spirit so as to form one body—whether Jews or Gentiles, slave or free—and we were all given the one Spirit to drink" (1 Cor. 12:12–13). Paul compares the human body, which is one in spite of its many members, to the church, the body of Christ (v. 12). Though the church has many members, it is one body. Why? Because all members of the church participate in one Holy Spirit when they are incorporated into Christ's body. These are two different ways—sharing in the Spirit and being made a member of Christ's body—to describe the same reality: union with Christ.

Paul then uses two images, baptism and drinking, to teach that the Spirit connects believers to Christ (v. 13). The apostle first depicts Christ as baptizing believers with the Holy Spirit to incorporate them into Christ's body. His second picture is that "we were all given the one Spirit to drink" (v. 13). Witherington explains both pictures: "There are no Christians without the Spirit. At conversion the Christian is united to the body by the Spirit and is given the Spirit to drink."[7] The Holy Spirit is the bond of union with Christ.

The Spirit brings about the aspects of salvation that occur in union with Christ. The Holy Spirit is the person of the Godhead who joins believers to Christ. Therefore, it should not surprise us to find the Spirit active in uniting us to Christ. Union is the larger category, and the following elements flow from union with Christ: regeneration, justification, adoption, sanctification, and glorification. Each one occurs because we are united to Christ, and each one is brought about by the Spirit.

Against the backdrop of spiritual death Paul accents *regeneration*, that is, God making sinners alive to him: "But because of his great love for us, God, who is rich in mercy, made us alive with Christ even when we were dead in transgressions—it is by grace you have been saved" (Eph. 2:4–5). Regeneration takes place in union with Christ—"God . . . made us alive with Christ" (v. 4–5).

And this regeneration is the work of the Holy Spirit. The Spirit applies regeneration to those spiritually dead so that they come alive to God. Jesus says, "You should not be surprised at my saying, 'You must be born again.' The wind blows wherever it pleases. You hear its sound, but you cannot tell where it comes from or where it is going. So it is with everyone born of the Spirit'" (John 3:7–8). Jesus makes a word play: the same word (*pneuma*) means "breath, wind, or spirit." He likens the Holy Spirit's effects to those of the wind. The wind is free and beyond human control; it blows where it wants, and we cannot figure out its course ahead of time. We only know where it has been by its effects. So are those "born of the Spirit" (v. 8). The Holy Spirit acts in regeneration to unite us to Christ and bring us new life.[8]

Paul makes the connection between *justification* and union with Christ apparent in 2 Corinthians 5. Before speaking of justification, the apostle treats reconciliation (i.e., peace-making). Paul explains how God reconciles sinners to himself: "God made him who had no sin to be sin for us, so that in him we might become the righteousness of God" (v. 21). This is the language of justification. The righteous Christ became sin in God's sight so that we sinners might become God's righteousness. Our sin is imputed, or reckoned, to Christ, and his righteousness is imputed to us.

Paul writes, "God made him who had no sin to be sin for us, so that *in him* we might become the righteousness of God." Although rarely in Paul's writings do the words *in him* indicate union with Christ without further nuance, here they do so. Even as Christ shared in the plight of sinners to the point of dying (vicariously) as a sinner, so believers are declared righteous by God when they believe in Christ and share in his perfect righteousness.[9]

We see in 1 Corinthians 6, for example, that justification is the work of the Holy Spirit. After Paul condemns sinful lifestyles (v. 9), he encourages believers: "And that is what some of you *were*" (v. 11). Some of the Corinthian Christians had pursued these lifestyles before they believed. Paul continues, "But you were washed, you were sanctified, you were justified" (v. 11). He uses three verbs to describe their salvation. They were "washed" from the pollution of their sins, probably a reference to baptism. They were "sanctified" with initial or definitive sanctification, that powerful work of the Holy Spirit in constituting sinners as saints in Christ. They were "justified," or declared righteous, by the Father on the basis of Christ's saving work.

The two prepositional phrases that follow are key: "in the name of the Lord Jesus Christ" and "by the Spirit of our God" (v. 11). The two phrases probably apply to all three verbs, but they certainly go with the final verb—"justified." So what is the connection between justification and "the name of the Lord Jesus

Christ"? We are justified by believing in Christ's name. How were they "justified . . . by the Spirit of our God"? The Spirit enables us to believe in Christ's name. The Spirit grants the gift of saving faith, enabling sinners to believe in Jesus's name for justification, which is inseparable from union with Christ (2 Cor. 5:21). In conclusion, the Holy Spirit acts in justification to unite us to Christ and to bring us forgiveness and a righteous standing before God.

Adoption takes place in union with Christ. "So in Christ Jesus you are all children of God through faith, for all of you who were baptized into Christ have clothed yourselves with Christ" (Gal. 3:26–27). Being "baptized into Christ" denotes union with Christ, as the image of putting on clothes suggests. Baptism/conversion involves figuratively putting on Christ as one puts on clothes. The word *for* is important because it presents union with Christ, signified by baptism, as the reason God adopts believers.

Furthermore, adoption is the work of the Holy Spirit. Paul teaches that God's children are identifiable. They acknowledge the Holy Spirit's leadership and live for their heavenly Father (Rom. 8:14). Next, Paul contrasts the "spirit of slavery" and the "Spirit of adoption": "For you did not receive the spirit of slavery to fall back into fear, but you have received the Spirit of adoption as sons" (v. 15 ESV). God assures us of his fatherly love by giving us the Spirit.

Paul's next words present the Holy Spirit as the agent of adoption: "You have received the Spirit of adoption as sons, by whom we cry, 'Abba! Father!'" (v. 15). It is the Spirit who enables sinners to cry out for salvation to God as Father. Adoption, then, is the Spirit's work. He enables those who were enslaved to sin to believe in the unique Son and so become sons themselves. He enables them to call God "Father," "Abba," the same word Jesus uses to address his Father (Mark 14:36). By God's grace and the Spirit's agency believers have a relationship with God akin to Jesus's relationship to his Father. The Holy Spirit acts in adoption to unite us to Christ and bring us all the rights, privileges, and responsibilities that accompany it.

Sanctification too takes place in union with Christ. Sanctification involves dying to sin and living a new life for God. We die to sin when we are baptized: "Or don't you know that all of us who were baptized into Christ Jesus were baptized into his death?" (Rom. 6:3). Baptism denotes union with Christ in his death. We are baptized into Christ; we take part in his narrative. As he died, then, we also die to sin as we are united to Christ. Christ's atonement breaks the domination of sin over us; we no longer have to obey that harsh master. Instead, we belong to another Master, who bought us with his death and resurrection.

In addition, we are joined to Christ's resurrection. "We were therefore buried with him through baptism into death in order that, just as Christ was raised from the dead through the glory of the Father, we too may live a new life" (v. 4). We must live, then, as those who died to sin with Christ and who live to God. So Paul commands, "Do not offer any part of yourself to sin as an instrument of wickedness, but rather offer yourselves to God as those who have been brought from death to life; and offer every part of yourself to him as an instrument of righteousness" (v. 13).

This sanctification, like so many other acts in union with Christ, is the work of the Holy Spirit. Paul says that he, Silvanus, and Timothy "ought always to thank God for you, brothers and sisters loved by the Lord, because God chose you as firstfruits to be saved through the sanctifying work of the Spirit and through belief in the truth" (2 Thess. 2:13). Paul's ministry team should thank God always for loving and electing the Thessalonians for salvation. Paul specifies that God chose them "to be saved through the sanctifying work of the Spirit and through belief in the truth." Here are the means God uses to bring his plan into effect. He uses the Spirit's sanctifying work and the Thessalonians' resultant faith in the gospel to rescue them from their sins. The Holy Spirit acts in sanctification to join us to Christ, constitute us as saints, and begin the lifelong process of making us holy.

After teaching that the Spirit testifies within believers' hearts that God is their Father (Rom. 8:16), Paul extends the adoption metaphor to *glorification* by discussing our adoptive family's inheritance: "Now if we are children, then we are heirs—heirs of God and co-heirs with Christ" (v. 17). As God's children by adoption we are also his heirs! If we take into account the Bible's big story, the inheritance of believers is staggering: we inherit the Trinity and the new earth (1 Cor. 3:21–23 ESV; Rev. 21:1–7)! Because we are joined to Christ in his death, "we share in his sufferings" (Rom. 8:17). Because we are joined to Christ in his resurrection, we will "also share in his glory" (v. 17).

Furthermore, glorification is the work of the Holy Spirit. Scripture presents this truth indirectly in 1 Peter 4:13–14. Peter encourages persecuted believers to persevere in their faith by entrusting themselves to God and doing his will (5:12). Moreover, believers can even rejoice in persecution. "But rejoice inasmuch as you participate in the sufferings of Christ, so that you may be overjoyed when his glory is revealed" (1 Peter 4:13). Peter instructs his readers to be glad when they suffer for Christ now, because such suffering is an indication that they will share in his glory at his return. Underlying this verse is the doctrine of union with Christ in his past suffering and future glory.

This is where the Holy Spirit enters the picture: "If you are insulted because of the name of Christ, you are blessed, for the Spirit of glory and of God rests on you" (v. 14). When believers suffer for being Christians, they can rejoice because they have been joined to Christ and thereby participate in the Spirit. The way that Peter refers to the Spirit here implies that glorification is the Spirit's work. New Testament scholar Peter Davids warrants quotation: "Thus those suffering for Christ experience through the Spirit now the glory they are promised in the future (1:7; 5:4; cf. 2 Cor. 4:17; Col 3:4). Indeed their very suffering is a sign that the reputation (glory) of God is seen in them, that the Spirit rests on them. They can indeed count themselves blessed."[10]

Peter, then, promises suffering believers a share "when his [Christ's] glory is revealed" in verse 13 and then speaks of "the Spirit of glory and of God" resting on them in verse 14. The implication is that the "Spirit of glory" will enable each one of them to "share in the glory to be revealed" (5:1). Therefore, "the Spirit of glory and of God" (4:14) will act in glorification to unite believers to Christ "when his glory is revealed" (v. 13).

The Holy Spirit is sometimes referred to as the forgotten person of the Trinity for he is not as prominent in Scripture as the Father and Son. The Spirit is the servant of the other two divine persons and brings them glory. The Spirit deserves more attention than he usually receives. He is a divine person, equal to the Father and Son in power and glory. He performs works that only God can, in creation, Scripture, the world, the apostles, and Jesus. In fact, he was active in Jesus's life from his conception to his inauguration of the church.

Most important for our purposes are the facts that the Spirit is indispensable to and applies salvation. The Spirit joins believers to Christ and salvation from beginning to end. Here is where the Spirit provides real help to those who struggle with assurance. In chapter 1 (pp. 25–26) we met William Lobdell, the religion reporter whose faith was destroyed by the hypocrisy of sex scandals in the Catholic Church and unethical behavior in the evangelical community. As in most cases, there are no easy answers for Lobdell's questions. But if he found a warm and nurturing Christian community that practiced what it preached, perhaps he could begin to recover. He needs people who love him because God first loved them in Christ, who loved us and gave himself for us. Sincere believers, filled with Spirit, could point Lobdell to the same Spirit who assures them of God's love. In the next chapter, we will see that it is the Spirit who assures God's people of his love for them.

CHAPTER 6

THE HOLY SPIRIT'S ROLE IN ASSURANCE

The Spirit's ministry as witness is an important part of the story of Christian assurance. . . . The main part of the story of assurance . . . lies in the finished work of Christ upon the cross. Furthermore, the subjective correlate to that objective work of the cross is our faith. Faith is a necessary condition for the experience of salvation. No faith, no assurance. The witness of the Spirit and exhibition of good works are secondary and corroborative. . . . But how can we be sure that we are adopted children of God? The Spirit is the answer. The Spirit jointly bears witness with our spirits . . . that we are children of God.[1]

Graham Cole teaches biblical truths in proper proportion, as the above quote shows. The chief basis of assurance is the gospel of Jesus's saving death and resurrection. And the gospel must be received by faith. Good works and the Spirit's witness are key ways that God assures us, but they are secondary to the gospel. Having previously examined God's promises of salvation and preservation, we are ready to learn more about the Spirit's role in assuring Christians.

In at least five texts the New Testament teaches that the Holy

Spirit assures believing hearts. I will combine the three passages from 1 John under one heading:

- The Spirit's inner witness to God's love (Romans 5:1–5)
- The Spirit's inner witness to our adoption (Romans 8:14–17)
- The Spirit's inner witness to abiding (1 John 3:19–24; 4:13–16; 5:6–12)

THE SPIRIT'S INNER WITNESS TO GOD'S LOVE (ROMANS 5:1-5)

God assures us of salvation by the Holy Spirit's ministry in our hearts: "God's love has been poured out into our hearts through the Holy Spirit, who has been given to us" (Rom. 5:5). Before we look at the Spirit's inner assurance of God's love, let's clear up a common misunderstanding concerning God's love and consider the love of the Trinity.

God Is Love

Amazingly, Scripture affirms that "God is love" (1 John 4:8, 16). Unfortunately, this concept has been misunderstood in various ways. Some have claimed it means that love is God's chief quality, to be placed above all his other qualities. But this is absurd. Is God more loving than he is holy? Or more loving than he is wise? Or more loving than he is powerful? Or more loving than he is faithful? To ask these questions is to answer them. God possesses all his qualities in equal measure. He is altogether loving, holy, wise, powerful, faithful, etc.

The biblical truth that God is love has been abused when it is set against his other qualities. Everyone will be saved in the end, we are told, because God is love, and his love trumps his holiness and justice. This too is a misunderstanding because before 1 John tells us God is love it declares "God is light; in him there is no darkness at all" (1:5). This is not to say that God is more light than love; we have already pronounced such an idea absurd.

But neither is he more love than light. God is holy and loving. He is holy love, or compassionate holiness. His qualities are inseparable from his identity.

For this reason Scripture teaches that Christ has to come and make atonement for sins. This was the loving God's way of dealing with sin so we could come to know him. God's holiness offended by our sins demanded satisfaction. Christ's cross-work enabled God to be holy love and still forgive our sins (Rom. 3:25–26). It enabled him to maintain his moral integrity and rescue all who trust Christ as Lord and Savior.

What does Scripture teach when it declares twice in short compass that God is love (1 John 4:8, 16)? It means that love is an inherent quality of God (along with his other qualities). Part of what it means for God to be God is for him to love the world. This active will to love is supremely displayed in the Father sending his Son to be Savior of the world (4:9–10, 14).

The Father, Son, and Holy Spirit Love Us

Holy Scripture abundantly proclaims the love of God the Father, Son, and Holy Spirit. Almost thirty texts broadcast the Father's love. Here is a sample:

> For God so loved the world that he gave his one and only Son, that whoever believes in him shall not perish but have eternal life. (John 3:16)

> But God demonstrates his own love for us in this: While we were still sinners, Christ died for us. (Rom. 5:8)

> But because of his great love for us, God, who is rich in mercy, made us alive with Christ even when we were dead in transgressions—it is by grace you have been saved. (Eph. 2:4–5)

> See what great love the Father has lavished on us, that we should be called children of God! (1 John 3:1)

This is love: not that we loved God, but that he loved us and sent his Son as an atoning sacrifice for our sins. (4:10)

Scripture also abundantly declares the love of God the Son for us. This occurs in close to twenty texts, of which the following is a selection:

As the Father has loved me, so have I loved you. (John 15:9)

The life I now live in the body, I live by faith in the Son of God, who loved me and gave himself for me. (Gal. 2:20)

And I pray that you, being rooted and established in love, may have power, together with all the Lord's holy people, to grasp how wide and long and high and deep is the love of Christ, and to know this love that surpasses knowledge (Eph. 3:17–19)

This is how we know what love is: Jesus Christ laid down his life for us. And we ought to lay down our lives for our brothers and sisters. (1 John 3:16)

To him who loves us and has freed us from our sins by his blood . . . to him be glory and power for ever and ever! Amen. (Rev. 1:5–6)

Scripture also proclaims the love of God the Holy Spirit, but not as extensively as that of the Father and the Son. This is in keeping with the Spirit's role as their servant. Some theological explanation may help. In the treatment of the life of the Trinity in the New Testament, there is a stress on the Father's love for the Son and the Son's love for the Father, but not on the Spirit's love for the Father and the Son. According to the church fathers (an insight that goes back to Augustine[2]) the Spirit's role is to bind Father and Son together in love. Likewise, then, in the New Testament the stress is on the Father's love for believers and on the Son's love for believers. The Spirit's role, on the other hand, in keeping with the way of the divine life, is to bind God's people together in love with one another and with him. This tends to be the emphasis with regard to the Spirit's role in such texts as the following:

> May the grace of the Lord Jesus Christ, and the love of God, and the fellowship of the Holy Spirit be with you all. (2 Cor. 13:14)[3]

> You learned it from Epaphras, our dear fellow servant, who is a faithful minister of Christ on our behalf, and who also told us of your love in the Spirit. (Col. 1:7–8)[4]

> And hope does not put us to shame, because God's love has been poured out into our hearts through the Holy Spirit, who has been given to us. (Rom 5:5)

The latter is such an important text we will look at it further below. Here another theological point must be made about the Spirit's love for us. While each member of the Trinity plays unique roles in God's economy, it is also true that in every act of God all three members of the Trinity are involved. So when the Scriptures say that the Father loves us or the Son loves us, it is understood that the Spirit loves us as well.

The Spirit's love for believers seems to rest behind texts that speak of the harm done to the Holy Spirit by those who are unfaithful:

> And do not grieve the Holy Spirit of God, with whom you were sealed for the day of redemption. (Eph. 4:30)[5]

> How much more severely do you think someone deserves to be punished who has trampled the Son of God under-foot, who has treated as an unholy thing the blood of the

covenant that sanctified them, and who has insulted the Spirit of grace? (Heb. 10:29)[6]

God is love, and God the Father, Son, and Holy Spirit love the people of God. So it does not surprise us that God graciously pours out this love in our hearts through the Holy Spirit.

Romans 5:1–5

Therefore, since we have been justified through faith, we have peace with God through our Lord Jesus Christ, through whom we have gained access by faith into this grace in which we now stand. And we boast in the hope of the glory of God. Not only so, but we also glory in our sufferings, because we know that suffering produces perseverance; perseverance, character; and character, hope. And hope does not put us to shame, because God's love has been poured out into our hearts through the Holy Spirit, who has been given to us.

Romans 5:1–11 wonderfully combines the three ways God assures his people of salvation. Since I will treat this passage in chapter 8, I will merely list the other two ways here and focus on the Spirit's inner witness. God assures us through the promise of the gospel to save (vv. 1–2, 6–8, 11) and keep (vv. 6–10) us. He also assures us by working in our lives (vv. 3–4).

God also kindly assures his people of final salvation by the Holy Spirit's work in their hearts. After saying that God gives his people confidence of a future salvation that they cannot see by working in them now what they can see (vv. 3–4), Paul affirms that such hope of ultimate salvation "does not put us to shame" (v. 5). The basis for this statement? "God's love has been poured out into our hearts through the Holy Spirit, who has been given to us" (v. 5).

God has declared his love to us outside us in the gospel, as the many passages rehearsing the Trinity's love for us above testify. I am convinced that that external basis of assurance is most significant. But it does not stand alone. God also bears witness inside us. He gives an internal witness of our salvation in the person of the Holy Spirit.

Indeed, God the Father assures us of his love within us. The Father pours out his love, as it were, into our hearts through the Spirit. This is the first mention of God's love in Romans, and the verses following develop the idea. In verses 6–8 Paul asserts that God's love is undeserved, based on his initiative, and active. We did not merit God's love; we deserved his wrath. We did not first love him, but he us. Moreover, his love is not passive; he sent Christ to rescue us.

Our hope of eternal life is not illusory for God has graciously, abundantly, and internally assured us of it. God is gracious; we have no claim on his love. He voluntarily loves us. He does so abundantly as the verb "poured out" suggests. James Dunn likens this to a "cloudburst on a parched countryside."[7] God comforts us internally; he pours out his love *"into our hearts."* God causes his people to experience his love. God effects "this word at the level of their motive and emotive center . . . 'our inmost heart'— NEB."[8] Amazingly, the Holy Spirit performs this ministry: "God's love has been poured out into our hearts *through the Holy Spirit* who has been given to us." In fulfillment of Old Testament prophecies of the New Covenant, the Spirit was poured out at Pentecost. Schreiner captures the apostle's thought:

> The gift of the Holy Spirit demonstrates that believers will be spared from God's wrath in the day of judgment. In particular, through the Spirit believers have experienced the love of God in their hearts. . . . We should not make any sharp distinction between the love of God and the Holy Spirit. . . . the Spirit has the unique ministry of filling believers with the love of God. What Paul refers to here is the dynamic experience of the Spirit in one's life. . . . Believers know now in their hearts that they will be spared from God's wrath because they presently experience God's love for them through the ministry of the Holy Spirit.[9]

God is very gracious to us rebels. He reaches out to us in love through the gospel. He causes it to fall on our ears, and he works in our hearts that we might believe it. The gospel carries assurance with it. Its promise of forgiveness and assurance strengthen our hearts for judgment day. We know now that we are saved and safe from hell. Not only so! In addition to the gospel's assurance outside us, God witnesses to his love within us. Specifically he lavishes his love on us internally by his Spirit. He causes us to experience his love, announced without in the gospel, within by his Spirit. God thus grants confidence of final salvation without and within.

THE HOLY SPIRIT'S INNER WITNESS TO OUR ADOPTION: ROMANS 8:14-17

For those who are led by the Spirit of God are the children of God. The Spirit you received does not make you slaves, so that you live in fear again; rather, the Spirit you received brought about your adoption to sonship. And by him we cry, "*Abba*, Father." The Spirit himself testifies with our spirit that we are God's children. Now if we are children, then we are heirs—heirs of God and co-heirs with Christ, if indeed we share in his sufferings in order that we may also share in his glory.

Here the Holy Spirit's ministry of assuring believers is expressed in the language of adoption. Before explaining this passage, I will summarize Scripture's teaching on the warm doctrine of adoption. Paul did not treat adoption in isolation. He employed it as an extended metaphor to talk about everything from God to last things. We will look at these topics in turn.

A Theology of Adoption

The Holy Trinity loves the people of God. The names of the first two persons of the Trinity are well suited to express God's love for his people in terms of adoption. Their names are familial: God the Father and God the Son. The name "the Holy Spirit" is not as well suited for this task. So what does God do? He alters the name of the third person of the Trinity! He is called "the Spirit of his [the Father's] Son" (Gal. 4:6) and "the Spirit of adoption" (Rom. 8:15 ESV). Each of the Trinitarian persons loves us and plays a role in our adoption.

The Father plays an important part: "In love he predestined us for adoption to sonship through Jesus Christ, in accordance with his pleasure and will—to the praise of his glorious grace" (Eph. 1:4–6). Our adoption is rooted in the Father's love and will. He adopted us because he loved us and chose us. Before creation (v. 4) he planned to adopt us. His plan was to do this "through Jesus Christ," his Son. The Father planned to send Jesus as the Mediator, whose death and resurrection would result in multitudes becoming God's children. The Father adopts believers in his unique Son into his family as the Spirit enables them to call God "Father" in truth. Further, all of this Trinitarian activity is "to the praise of" God's "glorious grace" (v. 6).

Human beings were created in God's image and are his children by creation. But the fall of our first father Adam ruined our relationship with God. As a result fallen people are "in slavery under the elemental spiritual forces of the world" (Gal. 4:3). Unknown to them, lost persons are subject to the realm of the demonic. They are "the children of the devil" (1 John 3:10) and unwittingly obey him. Only in Christ do they become "the children of God" (v. 10). Only in Christ can it be said of them: "So you are no longer a slave, but God's child" (Gal. 4:7). So, from the perspective of adoption, lost persons are slaves of sin in dire need of a Redeemer.

Christ is the unique Son of God by nature. He is the eternal Son of God. There was never a time when the Father did not have a Son or the Son a Father. Their relationship is eternal. Jesus says to the Father, "You loved me before the creation of the world" (John 17:24). Scripture teaches that the eternal Son of God became incarnate to rescue rebels. In doing so the Son became adopted in a new sense. As the representative Man, the second Adam, he arose from the grave and was vicariously adopted (Acts 13:32–33; Rom. 1:3–4).[10] The Father proclaimed him Son who loved us, gave himself for us, and overcame death in his resurrection. When we are joined to Christ by faith, his sonship becomes ours; we become God's sons or daughters in him.

By contrast human beings, though God's children by creation, since the fall are by nature slaves to sin. By grace through faith in the unique Son believers become the sons or daughters of God (Gal. 3:26; John 1:12). The Father adopts them into his family as adult children.[11]

Christ's saving work, viewed from the perspective of adoption, accomplishes redemption. His death on the cross purchases slaves so they become sons: "God sent his Son, born of a woman, born under the law, to redeem those under the law, that we might receive adoption to sonship" (Gal. 4:4–5). Paul explains the form this work of redemption takes: "Christ redeemed us from the curse of the law by becoming a curse for us, for it is written: 'Cursed is everyone who is hung on a pole'" (3:13). The holy Son of God took the penalty of the law—its curse—for us that we might be redeemed and receive God's blessing rather than a curse (v. 14).

Like justification, adoption is by grace through faith in Christ: "in Christ Jesus you are all children of God, through faith" (Gal. 3:26). John teaches the same thing: "Yet to all who did receive him [Christ], to those who believed in his name, he gave the right to become children of God" (John 1:12).

The Spirit plays key roles, to which we will turn when we finish this survey of adoption.

The Christian life is a life of knowing God as our Father and Christ as our Brother. It is difficult for God requires that "we share in his sufferings in order that we may also share in his glory" (Rom. 8:17). But it is also a life of fellowship with the Spirit of adoption who testifies to God's love in our hearts (v. 16).

From the perspective of adoption, the church is the family of God. Baptism and the Lord's Supper are family ceremonies. The former is the rite of initiation into the family and the latter is the family fellowship meal. Church discipline is family discipline.[12]

Adoption teaches much about last things too. Since believers are sons, they are also heirs, "if we are children, then we are heirs—heirs of God and co-heirs with Christ" (Rom. 8:17). In fact, their status has undergone a complete reversal. If you trust Christ as Redeemer, "you are no longer a slave, but God's child; and since you are his child, God has made you also an heir" (Gal. 4:7). As believers live for God in a sinful world, struggling with their and others' sins, we "groan inwardly as we wait eagerly for our adoption to sonship, the redemption of our bodies" (Rom. 8:23). In the resurrection we will "be conformed to the image of his Son" in glory (v. 29).

The Holy Spirit's Role
The Gift of Faith

Adoption, then, is an extended metaphor by which Paul teaches us about our identity in Christ and how God wants us to live. He does not omit the Holy Spirit. The Spirit plays two roles in adoption. He is "the agent through whom the believer's sonship is both bestowed and confirmed."[13] First, the Spirit enables us to cry out to God in saving faith: "The Spirit you received does not make you slaves, so that you live in fear again; rather, the Spirit you received brought about your adoption to sonship. And by him we cry, '*Abba*, Father'" (Rom. 8:15). The Spirit gives the gift of saving faith to God's people. It is the Spirit's "work of enabling us to believe in Jesus Christ, through whom alone we may rightly call God 'Father.'"[14] As the Spirit works in our hearts, God replaces fear with trust, peace, and security.

It is essential to note the import of the word *Abba* here, for it is one feature that makes adoption so endearing. James Dunn's words bear repeating:

It is generally accepted that "Abba" was characteristic and distinctive of Jesus' own prayer life. . . . It is . . . justified to assert that Jesus' use of "Abba" most probably implies a sense of intimate sonship on the part of Jesus, expressed as it was in the colloquial language of close family relationship. . . . It attests that this language was remembered as that of Jesus: it is precisely because believers found themselves crying to God with the word used by Jesus that they could be sure that they shared in Jesus' sonship and inheritance (vv. 16–17).[15]

The Internal Witness

Second, the Spirit assures all believers of God's love and their sonship: "The Spirit himself testifies with our spirit that we are God's children" (v. 16). This is the internal witness of the Spirit. God ministers assurance of salvation to us in three main ways. First, he uses his Word to assure us. Both his promises to save us (the gospel) and to keep us (preservation) give us confidence of final salvation. Second, God works in our lives to assure us. He motivates us to love and serve him, convicting us increasingly of our sins. Third, and most significant at present: God mysteriously testifies deep in our hearts that he is our Father and we are his children.

In an extensive passage on adoption (Gal. 3:26–4:7) Paul speaks similarly: "Because you are his sons, God sent the Spirit of his Son into our hearts, the Spirit who calls out, 'Abba, Father'" (4:6). This passage accentuates the roles of the Trinity in adoption. The Father sent the Son, born of the Virgin Mary and accountable to God's law, to perform the work of redemption no one else could perform. As God he was able to save his people from their sins. As the God-man, he obeyed the law perfectly and died for the sake of his people. His accursed death redeems them from the curse of the law and the bondage of sin (3:13; 4:4, 6). As a result those who by God's grace believe in Christ the Redeemer "receive adoption to sonship" (4:5). And to them "God sent the Spirit of his Son into our hearts, the Spirit who calls out, 'Abba! Father'" (v. 6).

The Father sent the Spirit of his Son into believers' hearts. He is the Spirit of Christ because Christ, the anointed one, received the Spirit at his baptism so he could pour out the Spirit after his death, resurrection, and ascension. He did this on the day of Pentecost according to the Father's plan. The Father sent this "Spirit of his Son" into our hearts. For what purpose? Schreiner replies: "Paul introduces the sending of the Spirit to confirm that they are truly sons of God. . . . The point is that the Spirit confirms, authenticates, and ratifies their sonship."[16]

We note where the Father sent the Spirit—into Christians' hearts. Longenecker elucidates: "The use of . . . 'heart' as the seat of a person's intellectual and emotional life generally . . . and as the center of one's moral and spiritual life in particular . . . is common in biblical thought."[17] It is even more critical to be clear on the primary purpose of the Holy Spirit in the life of believers. Again Longenecker helps:

> The primary function of the Spirit in one's life, however, is not to cause a believer in Jesus to become a "spiritual" or "charismatic" person, as is so often popularly assumed, but to witness to the filial relation of the believer with God that has been established by the work of Christ—a witness both to the believer (so 3:2, 5) and to God the Father (so here).[18]

In other words, the Spirit gives assurance of sonship. Schreiner agrees: "The fundamental proof and evidence that the Galatians are truly God's adopted sons is that God has given them the Holy Spirit, and their sonship is expressed by their acclamation that God is their Father. . . . And the Galatians know they are truly believers, for the Spirit confirms it in their hearts."[19]

In sum: although the words of Galatians 4:6 and Romans 8:15–16 differ, their messages overlap. "It is the Spirit who cries out to God the Father on behalf of the believer, though synonymously Paul can also say that the believer cries out to God the Father as energized by the Spirit (Rom. 8:15)," as Longenecker notes.[20] And Paul's writing, "The Spirit himself testifies with our spirit that we are God's children" (v. 16), is similar. God loves us and wants us to know that he is ours and we are his. He tells us so in his Word, gives evidences of it in our lives, and testifies within by the Spirit that he is our Father and we are his children. Praise his holy name!

THE HOLY SPIRIT'S INNER WITNESS TO ABIDING IN 1 JOHN 3-5

Though not always recognized, the apostle John as well as Paul teaches that the Holy Spirit assures Christians of their relationship to God. John does so in his first epistle.

The Holy Spirit Testifies to God's Abiding in Us: 1 John 3:19-24

> This is how we know that we belong to the truth and how we set our hearts at rest in his presence: If our hearts condemn us, we know that God is greater than our hearts, and he knows everything. Dear friends, if our hearts do not condemn us, we have confidence before God and receive from him anything we ask, because we keep his commands and do what pleases him. And this is his command: to believe in the name of his Son, Jesus Christ, and to love one another as he commanded us. The one who keeps God's commands lives in him, and he in them. And this is how we know that he lives in us: We know it by the Spirit he gave us.

John begins: "This is how we know that we belong to the truth and how we set our hearts at rest in his presence" (v. 19). In context "This is" goes with the preceding. John defines love differently than contemporary Greeks or Jews: it is defined by Christ's laying down his life for us. John urges his readers to follow Christ's example and do the same for one another (v. 16). He rejects the profession of faith of a selfish person who sees a believer in need, has the means to help, and does nothing (v. 17). John exhorts his readers to love in action and not merely in words (v. 18). This shows the reality of our faith and strengthens our hearts (v. 19). Yarbrough is perceptive: "To love, then, in both word and deed is to know more clearly that the source of one's identity and life as a believer is the truth—which is to say, in John's frame of reference, Christ (John 14:6; cf. 1:14, 17; 8:32). John's first word of assurance points readers to Jesus."[21]

John adds, "This is . . . how we set our hearts at rest in his presence" (v. 19). Despite the self-evaluation called for by verses 16–18, readers can set their hearts at ease before God. They do so, despite their inability to fulfill the command to love perfectly, because they have the right heart attitude and show real but imperfect love for others. Even when they are aware of falling short, they can have assurance: "If our hearts condemn us, we know that God is greater than our hearts, and he knows everything" (v. 20). Even when our love for others is lacking, we can find solace in God's greatness and mercy. When our hearts are burdened with our sins, we dare not run from God but must turn to him in repentance, as Yarbrough explains:

> God's greatness is relevant to the state of the human heart. "God is greater than our hearts" for John, not in the sense that he so transcends them that there is no personal point of contact (as, e.g., with Allah in Islam), but in the sense that precisely as the exalted Lord, he ministers comfort to the individual. . . . If our conscience condemns, "God overrides the verdict."[22]

John says: "Dear friends, if our hearts do not condemn us, we have confidence before God and receive from him anything we ask, because we keep his commands and do what pleases him" (vv. 21–22). If our hearts condemn us, we run to our Father in repentance, and he comforts us in mercy. If our hearts do not condemn us, we remain confident in our relationship with our Father.

This confidence has two sides: we are assured of salvation and of answers to prayer. When we walk with God, we gain confidence that he answers our prayers. Loving and obeying God strengthens assurance: "we keep his commands and do what pleases him" (v. 22).

John says that God's command is: "to believe in the name of his Son, Jesus Christ, and to love one another as he commanded us" (v. 23). John writes to assure believing readers of eternal life (5:13). He does so by pointing to three evidences of that life in them: believing the right things about Jesus, obeying God, and loving one another. Here he combines all three. We are to obey God's command to believe in Jesus and love one another. This is characteristic as John interweaves themes and moves freely from one to another. Here this has the effect of stressing the affinity of faith, obedience, and love. They are evidences of the same thing— eternal life.

John ends this section by speaking of mutual abiding between believers and God and the Holy Spirit's assurance. He writes, "The one who keeps God's commands lives in him, and he in them" (v. 24). John says much about believers' warm relationship with God. He does so with the intimate language of mutual abiding, of living in one another. Obedient believers live in God and he in them. To grasp the language requires understanding of the Trinity. There is one God who eternally exists in three persons, Father, Son, and Holy Spirit. These three are distinct but inseparable. And they mutually indwell one another (John 14:10– 11). That is, each one of the Trinitarian persons is fully God. Now incredibly John teaches that believers in a sense participate in this reciprocal indwelling. This does not compromise the distinction between the Creator and his creatures. For, though the Trinity's mutual indwelling is eternal and by nature, our mutual indwelling of God is by grace through faith in Christ. Nevertheless, in both his gospel and first epistle, John says that believers live in God and he in them (John 17:21; 1 John 4:13–16).

What does the Spirit have to do with the assurance of which

John speaks in this passage? Much, for "this is how we know that he lives in us: We know it by the Spirit he gave us" (v. 24). As in verse 19, "this is" here refers backward. It points back to obedience to God's commands. The Spirit assures believers within when they obey God and love other believers. Yarbrough agrees: "Believers know, by the Spirit that God (or Christ) gives them, that they abide in Christ and Christ in them as they keep the commandments to trust and love."[23] The Spirit assures believers within that they abide in the Father and the Son and they in believers.

It is not unusual for believers' accusing consciences to question their relationship with God. We also can put so much pressure on ourselves to base assurance on our perfect obedience to God's commands that we doubt. John, therefore, points us to a more reliable source of confidence—the Spirit whom God gave us assures us that God lives in us. Like Paul, John regards the Spirit's present witness as a great comfort in the Christian life.

The Holy Spirit Testifies to Mutual Abiding: 1 John 4:13–16

This is how we know that we live in him and he in us: He has given us of his Spirit. And we have seen and testify that the Father has sent his Son to be the Savior of the world. If anyone acknowledges that Jesus is the Son of God, God lives in them and they in God. And so we know and rely on the love God has for us. God is love. Whoever lives in love lives in God, and God in them.

Again John links the Holy Spirit with assurance. He previously spoke of the Spirit's assuring Christians that God lives in them (3:24). Now he says that the Spirit gives believers confidence that God and they mutually abide: "This is how we know that we live in him and he in us: He has given us of his Spirit" (v. 13). "This is" seems to go with what follows.[24] Believers know that God abides in them and they abide in God because he has given them the Spirit. Once more the Spirit plays a part in our confidence of final salvation. It is essential to note, as the next verses imply, that the Spirit's inner witness is not apart from the Word of God. The Spirit agrees with the apostles' witness to Jesus's incarnation and saving work. As eye-witnesses of Jesus's resurrection, the apostles are foundational to New Testament faith. The Spirit testifies within those who believe "that the Father has sent his Son to be the Savior of the world" (v. 14).

The Trinity works together to save us. The Father sends the Son into the world. He lives sinlessly, dies for sinners, and rises, promising eternal life to all who trust him. The Spirit assures those who believe that they are in union with God and he is in union with them. Only believers in Christ need look for the Spirit's inner witness. He assures those who know Christ of God's abiding presence. God only lives in those who acknowledge that Jesus is God's unique Son (v. 15). And they also live in God. John attests that God is love. This explains why God sent his Son to rescue us. When we believe in Christ "we know and rely on the love God has for us" (v. 16). As a result we love others with God's love. God's work in our lives assures us that he is ours and we are his, and this assurance too is in concert with the Spirit, who loves and indwells us.

Once more Yarbrough hits the nail squarely on its head:

> In 1 John 4:13 John speaks of the Spirit's role in believers' assurance that God is indeed in their midst as they reach out to others with the divine love that has touched them. . . . The Spirit is the link, even agent, who permits believers to see this reciprocity for what it is: a token of God's very presence among them, assuring them of the veracity of the message they have received and the importance of the ethic they are being called to embrace.[25]

The Holy Spirit Testifies to Eternal Life in the Son
1 John 5:6–12

This is the one who came by water and blood—Jesus Christ. He did not come by water only, but by water and blood. And it is the Spirit who testifies, because the Spirit is the truth.

For there are three that testify: the Spirit, the water and the blood; and the three are in agreement. We accept human testimony, but God's testimony is greater because it is the testimony of God, which he has given about his Son. Whoever believes in the Son of God accepts this testimony. Whoever does not believe God has made him out to be a liar, because they have not believed the testimony God has given about his Son. And this is the testimony: God has given us eternal life, and this life is in his Son. Whoever has the Son has life; whoever does not have the Son of God does not have life.

In verses 1–5 John stresses the importance of faith in Jesus for salvation. Now he focuses on faith's content, what we must believe to be saved. Regeneration is the cause of faith (v. 1 ESV). By faith in Christ all those regenerated conquer the world-system opposed to God. Verse 5 is a bridge: "Who is it that overcomes the world? Only the one who believes that Jesus is the Son of God." John affirms that Jesus "came by water and blood" (v. 6). John puts signposts at the start and end of Jesus's earthly ministry. "Water" refers to Jesus's baptism that began his ministry. "Blood" refers to Jesus's atoning death on the cross (cf. 4:10). By repetition John emphasizes that Jesus lived and died in history (5:6). The apostle John writes to confirm these truths. He is not alone for "it is the Spirit who testifies, because the Spirit is the truth" (v. 6).

John associates truth with the Trinity. He connects the Father (4:23, 24; 17:17) and the Son (1:14, 17; 14:6; 18:37) with the truth but mostly links the Holy Spirit and the truth:

And I will ask the Father, and he will give you another advocate to help you and be with you forever—the Spirit of truth. (14:16–17)

When the Advocate comes, whom I will send to you from the Father—the Spirit of truth who goes out from the Father—he will testify about me. (15:26)

But when he, the Spirit of truth, comes, he will guide you into all the truth. He will not speak on his own; he will speak only what he hears, and he will tell you what is yet to come. (16:13)

We are from God, and whoever knows God listens to us; but whoever is not from God does not listen to us. This is how we recognize the Spirit of truth and the spirit of falsehood. (1 John 4:6)

And it is the Spirit who testifies, because the Spirit is the truth. (5:6)

The last quote is from the passage we are studying. Since John often joins the Spirit and the truth it is fitting for him to cite the Spirit as a witness to Jesus's baptism and crucifixion. John grounds faith (5:1–12) in history and truth. The Spirit, like the Father and the Son, is the truth and speaks the truth. Moses, Jesus, and Paul cite the confirmatory power of two or three witnesses (Deut. 19:15; Matt. 18:16; 2 Cor. 13:1). John does the same: "For there are three that testify: the Spirit, the water and the blood; and the three are in agreement" (1 John 5:7–8).

John points out that we frequently accept the word of human beings. How much more should we accept God's testimony about his Son (v. 9). To receive eternal life people must believe God's testimony to his Son. Unbelievers reject it and in effect call God a liar. For persons to be saved, they must internalize God's external witness in the water and the blood to which the Spirit testifies. Additionally, God himself by the Spirit bears internal witness to the truth of the gospel. "Whoever believes in the Son of God has the testimony in himself" (v. 10, ESV).[26]

Here John presents something akin to Paul's internal witness of the Spirit. The Spirit not only outwardly confirms the truths of Jesus's life, mission, and atoning death. He also inwardly assures us that Jesus is the Son of God and Savior of humankind. Reduced to fundamentals, here is the good news: "God has given us eternal life, and this life is in his Son" (v. 11). It follows, then, that "Whoever has the Son has life; whoever does not have the Son of God does not have life" (v. 12). The "haves" exercise childlike faith in Jesus to cleanse them from sin and grant them eternal life. Conversely, the "have-nots" reject Christ as Lord and Savior.

John, then, in three passages in 1 John teaches that the Holy Spirit bears witness to God's abiding in us, our mutual abiding in God, and our possessing eternal life in the Son of God, who accomplished salvation for us. The Spirit plays an important, if subordinate, role in assurance.

CONCLUSION

Paul teaches that God is merciful to erring human beings. He brings us the message of love and deliverance through those who have tasted his forgiveness in Christ. By his Spirit he gives us the gift of faith that we might know him. The gospel with its promise of forgiveness carries assurance with it. God also witnesses to his love internally by his Spirit. He causes us to experience his love, announced without in the gospel, within by his Spirit: "God's love has been poured out into our hearts through the Holy Spirit, who has been given to us" (Rom. 5:5).

Some Christians overemphasize the person and ministries of the Holy Spirit and others neglect them. The Bible's picture of assurance calls for better balance. Giving priority to the Word in assurance, it is proper for us to look within to the Spirit because Scripture points us in that direction. Many of us need to talk to the indwelling Spirit more and enjoy his inner testimony to our Father's love for us.

Adoption is a beautiful biblical picture of salvation applied to us. Along with the Father's role of choosing his children and the Son's role of redeeming them, the Spirit too plays a role. He is God's agent to grant and confirm our adoption. First, he enables us to cry out to God in saving faith: "the Spirit you received brought about your adoption to sonship. And by him we cry, 'Abba, Father'" (Rom. 8:15). Second, the Spirit of adoption assures us of our sonship: "The Spirit himself testifies with our spirit that we are God's children" (v. 16). This, the mysterious internal witness of the Spirit, convinces our hearts that God is our Father and we are his children.

Remember Steve from chapter 1 (pp. 22–23), whose sensitive heart and strong emotions sometimes lead him into spiritual turmoil where he questions his salvation? A spiritual doctor (a pastor) could prescribe Steve a strong dose of the doctrine of adoption as a partial remedy for his malady. Steve needs to meditate on Romans 8:14–17 and Galatians 3:26–4:7 and allow their truths to sink deep into his heart. Having believed the gospel, Steve should look for how the inner witness of the Spirit shows up in his heart (Rom. 8:16). He should not expect God to change his emotional make-up but should seek satisfaction in the knowledge and application of God's truth to his heart.

John too correlates the Spirit and assurance. The Spirit lets us know that Christ lives in us as we trust and obey him (1 John 3:24). Believers' accusing consciences and the pressure we put on ourselves to base assurance on performance raise doubts. We can be thankful that we have a more reliable source of confidence—the Spirit given by God assures us that God lives in us.

Believers know that God abides in them and they abide in God because he has given them the Holy Spirit (4:13). The Spirit's inner witness is not apart from the Word of God. The Spirit agrees with the apostles' witness to Jesus's incarnation and saving work (v. 14). And the Spirit's assurance of our mutual abiding with God moves us to share his love with others.

John calls the Spirit as a witness to Jesus's baptism ("the water") and crucifixion ("the blood"). The Spirit, like the Father and the Son, is the truth and only speaks truth. Since we accept people's witness, much more should we accept God's witness about his Son (5:9). The Spirit, the water, and the blood testify to Christ's person and work. To receive eternal life people must believe God's testimony to his Son. In addition, the Spirit bears internal witness to the truth of the gospel. "Whoever believes in the Son of God has the testimony in himself" (v. 10 ESV). Those who exercise childlike faith in Jesus have eternal life, but rejecters of Christ do not (v. 12).

Paul and John agree that the most critical basis of assurance is faith in the gospel, which carries with it God's promises to save and keep us. They also agree that the Spirit plays a vital corroborating internal role in giving Christians confidence on judgment day. Moreover, God assures his children in a third way—by working in their lives, a subject to which we now turn.

PART 3

ASSURANCE
AND THE
TRANSFORMED
LIFE

CHAPTER 7

THE ROLE OF GOOD WORKS

Robert N. Wilkin and the Grace Evangelical Society are convinced that good works play no part in assurance:

> If we believe the promise of everlasting life (e.g., John 3:16), then we are assured; it's that simple. We do not look to our works for assurance. We do not harbor hidden fears that we will appear at the final judgment only to find out we were never saved. Rather, we believe Jesus' promise that the one who believes in Him "has everlasting life [present tense], shall not come into judgment [future tense], but has passed from death into life [past tense]" (John 5:24). We rejoice in this security.[1]

Contrast Wilkin's view with that of the Puritans who titled a chapter of the Westminster Confession of Faith "Of Good Works":

> These good works, done in obedience to God's commandments, are the fruits and evidences of a true and lively faith: and by them believers manifest their thankfulness, strengthen their assurance, edify their brethren, adorn the

profession of the Gospel, stop the mouths of the adversaries, and glorify God whose workmanship they are.[2]

These views clash. Wilkin says, "We do not look to our works for assurance." Westminster says that good works "strengthen . . . assurance." The latter is the historic view of Protestantism, and for good reason, for Holy Scripture teaches it. I have presented the Word of God as the primary way God assures us of salvation, while affirming that Scripture teaches the Holy Spirit assures us internally. Here I round out the Bible's teaching on assurance by examining the role of good works. God saves sinners apart from works and then works in the lives of those who believe the gospel. I will treat four of the many passages that demonstrate this:

- Those doing the Father's will enter the kingdom: Matthew 7:21–23.
- Christians bear the fruit of the Spirit: Galatians 5:13–6:2.
- Christians must confirm their calling and election: 2 Peter 1:5–11.
- Christians walk in the light and confess their sins: 1 John 1:5–10.

THOSE DOING THE FATHER'S WILL ENTER THE KINGDOM: MATTHEW 7:21-23

False Prophets

After contrasting the small gate and narrow road leading to life, which few find, with the wide gate and broad road leading to destruction, which many enter, Jesus warns his disciples of false prophets. Although they appear to be harmless believers outwardly, inwardly they "are ferocious wolves," eager to devour the flock of God (Matt. 7:15). Twice Jesus enunciates an important principle for identifying false prophets: "By their fruits you will recognize them" (vv. 16, 20). Their sinful lives belie their profession of faith. Trees bear fruit according to their kind.

Healthy trees produce good fruit, and diseased trees produce bad fruit. False prophets, contrary to their claims and appearance, are bad trees fit only to "be cut down and thrown into the fire" (v. 19). Their sinful lifestyles show they are headed for eternal punishment.

False Disciples

Jesus then shifts his discussion from true and false prophets to true and false disciples. Once again, he teaches that poor performance reveals fraudulent claims:

> Not everyone who says to me, "Lord, Lord," will enter the kingdom of heaven, but only the one who does the will of my Father who is in heaven. Many will say to me on that day, "Lord, Lord, did we not prophesy in your name and in your name drive out demons and in your name perform many miracles?" Then I will tell them plainly, "I never knew you. Away from me, you evildoers!" (Matt. 7:21–23)

Jesus, playing the part of the judge on the last day, envisions some who profess to be his disciples confessing his lordship. This primitive Christian confession of Christ (v. 21; cf. Rom. 10:9; Phil. 2:11; 1 Cor. 12:3) is a good and necessary start. But verbal confession alone does not go far enough, and that is the point of these verses. Indeed, not all who make this claim will enter the final manifestation of the kingdom of heaven, only those who do the will of Jesus's heavenly Father. Mere profession of faith does not save. True confession of faith saves, and the lives of those who are truly saved provide evidence of their salvation. They know their heavenly Father and consequently do his will.

Mighty Deeds Do Not Save

Remarkably, Jesus explains how these false disciples will appeal to their prophecy, exorcisms, and miracles, all in Jesus's name, as evidence of their fitness to enter the kingdom (v. 22).

Jesus does not deny their claims. It is important to note that Jesus and his true disciples often performed these deeds. In spite of that Jesus only has harsh words for them: "I never knew you. Away from me, you evildoers!" (v. 23). Jesus never knew them in a personal saving relationship. Despite their performing mighty deeds in his name, they were never known savingly by Jesus. Instead of trusting him for the forgiveness of sins that would transform their lives, they remained in sin. Using the words of Psalm 6:8, Jesus repudiates them as "evildoers," as those who violated the Father's will.

Because those Jesus knows savingly do the Father's will, they gain assurance that they belong to him. Those whose lives are not characterized by doing the Father's will, "evildoers," should lack assurance and question whether they know the Lord. Regardless of whether they have supernatural experiences, true believers' lives are genuinely new, though not totally new. They are good trees that bear good fruit and thus show they are genuine believers. Their fruit, their lifestyle, confirms their profession of faith and contributes to their confidence that they possess salvation.

Some might protest that I am teaching salvation by works. Leon Morris effectively refutes this claim by explaining how Jesus's teaching challenges that notion:

> This is not salvation by works: the contrast is not between merit and grace, but between profession and way of life. If people really trust Christ for salvation, their lives will no longer be self-centered; that they belong to the good tree will be made manifest by the fruit they bear. The history of the church is replete with examples of ecclesiastics who made free use of expressions like "Lord, Lord," but whose arrogant and self-centered lives made a mockery of their words. Jesus is not saying that those saved will have earned their salvation, but that the reality of their faith will be made clear by their fruitful lives.[3]

CHRISTIANS BEAR THE FRUIT OF THE SPIRIT: GALATIANS 5:13–6:2

The acts of the flesh are obvious: sexual immorality, impurity and debauchery; idolatry and witchcraft; hatred, discord, jealousy, fits of rage, selfish ambition, dissensions, factions and envy; drunkenness, orgies, and the like. I warn you, as I did before, that those who live like this will not inherit the kingdom of God. But the fruit of the Spirit is love, joy, peace, forbearance, kindness, goodness, faithfulness, gentleness and self-control. Against such things there is no law. (Gal. 5:19–23)

Paul contrasts "the fruit of the Spirit" with "the acts of the flesh." Lives characterized by the former "belong to Christ Jesus" (v. 24). Lives characterized by the latter "will not inherit the kingdom of God" (v. 21). The apostle employs a chiastic pattern in 5:13–6:2 whereby he repeats his ideas in reverse order. Highlighting the elements of the chiasm illumines the passage:

    A. Command to love, 5:13–14
        B. Interpersonal abuses, 5:15
            C. Walk in the Spirit, 5:16–18
                D. Weeds, 5:19–21
                D. Fruit, 5:22–24
            C. Walk in the Spirit, 5:25
        B. Interpersonal abuses, 5:26
    A. Command to love, 6:1–2

The outer level of the pattern (A) consists of commands to love one another. This is explicit in verse 13 and implicit in 6:1–2, where Paul exhorts Christians to help the erring brother and so fulfill the law of Christ, which "is equivalent to the law of love (5:13–14)."[4]

Paul is upset that the Galatians are legalistic on two counts. First, they are entertaining a false gospel (1:6–9), which strikes at the vitals of the faith. Second, related to the first, they seem to have a legalistic view of the Christian life. Paul addresses this in the passage at hand. Here with mild sarcasm he tells them that the law's ethic is summarized in its command to love one another (v. 14). The Galatians' legalism was not producing overflowing love for one another, as the next level in the chiasm (B) shows. Instead, it was creating interpersonal abuses: infighting (5:15), pride, provocation, and jealousy (5:26).

Walking in the Spirit

What is the antidote to these interpersonal sins that are harming the Galatian churches? To walk in the Spirit, according to the chiasm's next level (C): verses 16 and 25. Verse 16 commands the readers to walk in the Spirit, and verse 25 urges them to do the same. What does it mean to walk in the Spirit? It means to rely on the Spirit step-by-step for the power to live the Christian life. Though the emphasis is on living by faith, walking in the Spirit is inseparable from obeying the Spirit. Let no one who deliberately and consistently disregards the Spirit claim to walk in the Spirit.

The inner level of the chiasm (D) takes us to the acts (or deeds) of the flesh and the fruit of the Spirit. Although there is not a one-to-one correspondence between the deeds and the fruit, the apostle intends us to understand them in opposition to one another. He explains, "For the flesh desires what is contrary to the Spirit, and the Spirit what is contrary to the flesh. They are in conflict with each other" (v. 17). It is profitable, therefore, to consider each deed in light of each fruit and vice versa.

Deeds of the Flesh

The "acts of the flesh" appear in four categories of sins: sexual, religious, interpersonal, and sins of excess:

- Sexual sins: sexual immorality, impurity, and debauchery (v. 19)
- Religious sins: idolatry and witchcraft (v. 20)

- Interpersonal sins: hatred, discord, jealousy, fits of rage, selfish ambition, dissensions, factions, and envy (vv. 20–21)
- Sins of excess: drunkenness, orgies, and the like (v. 21)

I will not comment on each act of the flesh, but some remarks are in order. Sexual and religious sins strike at our identities as human beings. We are gendered beings made to worship God. We go astray, and for us to counter these five sins, we must pursue purity of heart and love God with our entire being. It is no accident that interpersonal sins comprise the most extensive list because these were the sins ravaging the Galatian churches. These were the "fruit" of their legalistic approach to ethics. Sins of excess are characterized by a total lack of self-control. Paul is firm: "I warn you, as I did before, that those who live like this will not inherit the kingdom of God" (v. 21). Here the apostle warns, as he does elsewhere, that those whose lives are dominated by the acts of the flesh will not gain access to the future kingdom of God (cf. 1 Cor. 6:9–11; Eph. 5:5).

Fruit of the Spirit

Paul contrasts the fruit of the Spirit with the deeds of the flesh. Because of the interpersonal sins harming the congregation, he emphasizes those qualities that promote harmony. Love occupies first place on the list, adding to Paul's prior emphasis on loving one another. The infighting in the Galatian church will only be corrected as the Spirit increases love between its members. As this occurs, the rest of the fruit of the Spirit will become more visible among them. Their legalism has not produced much "joy, peace [among members], forbearance, kindness, goodness, faithfulness, gentleness and self-control [which opposes many acts of the flesh]" (vv. 22–23).

With a touch of sarcasm Paul adds, "Against such things there is no law" (v. 23). The law cannot produce this fruit; it is the work of the Spirit, who of course leads God's people to love and obey his law. The apostle then writes, "Those who belong to Christ

Jesus have crucified the flesh with its passions and desires" (v. 24). These words serve as both an encouragement and a warning. Christians are strengthened by the reminder that they have been joined to him spiritually in his crucifixion (2:20) and are therefore freed from the domination of their sinful desires. At the same time, these words warn any who profess the name of Christ yet whose lives are dominated by the acts of the flesh that they must make sure they know him whom they profess.

Assurance

Following the lead of John Sanderson, note that the gardening metaphor extends to Galatians 6:7–9, where the "acts of the flesh" appear as weeds.[5] What does Paul's teaching on the fruit of the Spirit contribute to our assurance of salvation? Much. First, when Paul speaks of the fruit of the Spirit, he means that the Spirit is the one producing the fruit (Gal. 5:22–23). As Thomas Schreiner says, "The godly qualities are the fruit of the Spirit, i.e., they are not the product of . . . human strength. . . . Believers are not called upon to summon up the strength within them, for their new way of life is supernatural, stemming from the powerful work of the Holy Spirit."[6] Thus in a passage in which he corrects the Galatians, he underscores the sovereignty of God in the Christian life. Our life for Christ is not a self-help program. At the same time he commands and exhorts his readers to walk in the Spirit (vv. 16, 25). We definitely play a part in the Christian life. Believers are not passive in living for Christ; we work hard under the lordship of Christ and the Spirit who empowers us (Col. 1:29; Phil. 2:12–13).

Second, Paul reminds us that because all believers have weeds in our gardens, we need the Holy Spirit's power to live a victorious Christian life. We are unable to conquer the deeds of the flesh on our own. We need the Spirit's power to pull the weeds and to do the ongoing work of cultivation. It is not a bad thing that we groan in our battle with sin; actually, it is a sign that we have the Spirit (Rom. 8:23). Don't forsake pulling weeds; doing so is a sign of spiritual life.

Third, we must distinguish between a garden with weeds and one overrun by weeds that has no fruit at all (v. 21). The former is the status of every Christian; the latter is a bad sign and may indicate a lack of salvation.

Fourth, the fruit must be understood over against the weeds. The fruit are character qualities that contribute to the health of the congregation. They are chiefly corporate, interpersonal, and their headwater is love, whose importance it is hard to overestimate. To overcome our sinful tendencies to harm others we must remember our cocrucifixion with Christ and our dependence on the Spirit for victory, for the fruit is his. God calls us to rely on and obey the Spirit while we walk step-by-step with him. God graciously strengthens our assurance as our brothers and sisters in Christ see his love, and the other fruits of the Spirit, in us. Even when the Spirit convicts us of a lack of fruit, if we turn to him, confess, and trust him more, we grow in assurance as we realize God has been at work in our lives.

CHRISTIANS MUST CONFIRM THEIR CALLING AND ELECTION: 2 PETER 1:5-11

Peter agrees that God strengthens assurance by working in believers' lives. He tells us to confirm our calling unto salvation and God's choice of us. We do this by practicing godly qualities.

> For this very reason, make every effort to add to your faith goodness; and to goodness, knowledge; and to knowledge, self-control; and to self-control, perseverance; and to perseverance, godliness; and to godliness, mutual affection; and to mutual affection, love. For if you possess these qualities in increasing measure, they will keep you from being ineffective and unproductive in your knowledge of our Lord Jesus Christ. But whoever does not have them is nearsighted and blind, forgetting that they have been cleansed from their past sins. Therefore, my brothers and sisters, make every effort

to confirm your calling and election. For if you do these things, you will never stumble, and you will receive a rich welcome into the eternal kingdom of our Lord and Savior Jesus Christ. (2 Peter 1:5–11)

In the preceding verses Peter taught that God gave believers all we need to live godly lives: his power and the promises of his Word. His goal is that we "may participate in the divine nature" (v. 4). This does not mean that we become divine. Rather we participate in God's nature by not indulging our evil desires and by becoming increasingly like him by his grace. Specifically, this means adding seven godly qualities to our faith in Christ. Peter's list is not prescriptive in its sequence, as if one virtue leads to the next. His list does have some order, however, for faith is first because saving faith is the prerequisite for the rest of the virtues, and love is last because it is the crown of the virtues (cf. Gal. 5:22; Col. 3:14; 1 Peter 1:22). We are to add moral virtue and increasing knowledge of God that comes from reading and obeying the Word. We are to add self-control and steadfastness, so as to finish our race with joy. In addition we are to add godliness, love for one another, and above all Christian love (2 Peter 1:5–7).

Growth in Character Qualities

Peter wants his readers to grow in their Christian lives—by cultivating these character qualities, by possessing "these qualities in increasing measure" (v. 8). He continues, "They will keep you from being ineffective and unproductive in your knowledge of our Lord Jesus Christ." He employs a figure of speech known as litotes, which uses a negative statement, usually an understatement, to make an affirmative one. When he says that these qualities will not make you "ineffective and unproductive," he means that possessing them will make us effective and productive. Peter's point is that growing in Christian character will cause our Christian lives to flourish. Peter has previously spoken of the knowledge of God (vv. 2, 3, 5). Here he teaches that if his hearers are growing in the

Christian virtues, they will be productive "in your knowledge of our Lord Jesus Christ." Peter means that they will grow in respect to salvation; they will mature as Christians.

Lack of Growth

As in the previous verse, so here Peter continues to speak about the Christian virtues of verses 5–7. After emphasizing the positive in verse 8, he now turns to the negative—if one of his readers "does not have" these qualities (v. 9). I regard it impossible to take these words absolutely. It is incomprehensible for a Christian to be described as totally lacking Christian character qualities. Since the latter part of this verse speaks of the person having his sins forgiven, I take this verse to speak of a genuine believer. I, therefore, do not take verse 9 to speak of people devoid of the virtues of verses 5–7 but to describe people who are not growing in Christ as Christians should. This was made clear in verse 8 by the phrase "in increasing measure." Their Christian lives are not flourishing. They are saved. They have experienced the forgiveness of sins. But they are not growing normally. They "lack these qualities" of which he just spoke (ESV).

Their malady is described two ways: as a vision problem and as forgetfulness. They have forgotten that their sins were forgiven. They have not properly remembered their identity in Christ. Another way of describing the same problem is to say that they are suffering from spiritual myopia, or nearsightedness. In this way they are "blind"; they lack the spiritual vision that comes from consistently walking with God. They are acting foolishly, not wisely. As implied by the previous verse, these people will not be productive or fruitful in their spiritual lives. In sum, growing in Christian character makes believers spiritually fruitful (v. 8); not growing in Christian character is foolish and makes them unfruitful (v. 9).

Confirming Our Calling and Election

Peter urges his readers toward spiritual zeal. Specifically, they are to "confirm" their "calling and election" (v. 10). Peter does not intend for us to confirm *to God* our calling and election, for "the Lord knows those who are his" (2 Tim. 2:19). Rather, Peter intends for us to confirm *for our benefit* our calling and election. They are to make sure God's calling them to salvation (cf. 1 Peter 1:3). This does not speak of the gospel call but of the effective call of God to his people, which occurs through the gospel call. They are to make certain that God chose them for salvation. By his calling them to himself in faith, they learn that he had chosen them before creation (Rom. 9:23–24; 1 Thess. 1:4–5). Thus by making certain their calling, they make certain their election.

In this verse Peter does not specify how his hearers are to make their salvation sure. The word *therefore* points us back to the previous verses. Peter urges his readers to gain assurance of salvation by cultivating the qualities of verses 5–7. The readers are to take pains to grow in Christian character. By doing so they become more confident of salvation. Moreover, by so doing they "will never stumble." Peter means they will never turn away from Christ; they will never trip in their faith and deny Christ.

Building upon the preceding verses Peter encourages his hearers. The phrase "for in this way" (v. 11 ESV) speaks of increasing in the Christian virtues mentioned above. By growing in character Peter's audience will richly inherit eternal life. They will live and die full of the assurance of salvation. Peter speaks of salvation in two ways in our passage. First, he tells of the "knowledge of our Lord Jesus Christ." Second, he speaks of entering "the eternal kingdom of our Lord and Savior Jesus Christ" (v. 11). Michael Green captures Peter's intention: "Words are piled upon one another to excite the weary pilgrim's heart at the splendour of that destination."[7]

This passage emphasizes Christians' responsibility to grow in faith by relying on God's power and trusting in his Word (vv. 3–4). They are "to make every effort" both to cultivate Christian character qualities (vv. 5–7) and "to confirm" their "calling and election" (v. 10). By doing these things they will never commit apostasy and will gain a rich entrance into the final dimension of the kingdom of Christ. Although our perseverance in living for Christ is not the basis of our assurance, the two are connected. Those who know the Lord, because they have tasted God's grace and trusted his Son for eternal salvation, live for God. By that same grace they grow in Christian virtues, thereby sharing in God's character, and increasing their assurance. By maturing in godly character qualities, they strengthen their assurance of salvation.

CHRISTIANS WALK IN THE LIGHT AND CONFESS THEIR SINS: 1 JOHN 1:5–10

John's purpose statement in his first epistle is straightforward: "I write these things to you who believe in the Son of God that you may know that you have eternal life" (1 John 5:13). John writes to assure believers of salvation. He repeatedly points to their faith, holiness, and love as evidence for believers' eternal life.

False Teachers

The churches John wrote to had been infiltrated by false teachers, who were trying to convince them of errors concerning Christ and the Christian life (1:8–10; 2:26; 4:1–5). When the false teachers failed to persuade the church, the teachers rejected John's readers and left them (2:18–19). Though they had weathered the storm of false doctrine, John's readers had been battered, and their assurance of salvation shaken. Into this situation John wrote to encourage and assure. He wanted to bolster his readers' confidence of salvation.

John tells his readers that their continuing in faith (3:21–24; 4:1–3), love (3:14; 4:16–18), and holiness (2:5–6; 3:10) confirms that they have eternal life. But before he writes these things, he makes his programmatic statement for the epistle. John's statement in 1 John 1:5–10 is foundational for all that follows. Understanding this passage not only helps us understand the rest of the epistle but also helps us understand the role of changed lives in Christian assurance.

This is the message we have heard from him and declare to you: God is light; in him there is no darkness at all. If we claim to have fellowship with him and yet walk in the darkness, we lie and do not live out the truth. But if we walk in the light, as he is in the light, we have fellowship with one another, and the blood of Jesus, his Son, purifies us from all sin. If we claim to be without sin, we deceive ourselves and the truth is not in us. If we confess our sins, he is faithful and just and will forgive us our sins and purify us from all unrighteousness. If we claim we have not sinned, we make him out to be a liar and his word is not in us. (1 John 1:5–10)

God Is Light

"This is the message we have heard from him and declare to you: God is light; in him there is no darkness at all" (v. 5). John and his fellow apostles pass on a crucial teaching from Jesus. Building on the Old Testament, John affirms that God is perfect light, utterly holy. Later he will add the equally important truth that "God is love" (4:8, 16). But he starts with light for good reason. God's character is the basis for everything John writes in this letter. God's absolutely holy nature is the ground for all John's ethical encouragements, exhortations, and warnings. Here too it provides the basis for exposing the false teachers' theological, moral, and relational darkness. In the five verses that follow, God's radiant light exposes "shadowy Christian belief, behavior, or devotion . . . as sham."[8]

In the next five verses, John uses five clauses beginning with the word *if* to distinguish living that corresponds to God's character from living that does not. According to John, the false teachers and those like them do not live for God and do not admit their sins. "If we claim to have fellowship with him and yet walk in the darkness, we lie and do not live out the truth" (v. 6). People claiming to have a close relationship with God ("fellowship") whose lives are characterized by sin are fooling themselves but not God. Since God is light and they are living in darkness, their behavior calls into question the genuineness of their profession of faith.

Walking in the Light

After John exposes this cheap faith, he encourages his readers: "But if we walk in the light, as he is in the light, we have fellowship with one another, and the blood of Jesus, his Son, purifies us from all sin" (v. 7). Those who know Christ live authentic lives, and they have fellowship with other authentic believers. Christians walking in the light of God enjoy him and each other. Does this mean that they are sinless? Does their godly walk make atonement for them? Both of these questions deserve a negative answer. Though Christians' lives are not typified by sin, Christians still sin. Christ's saving death and resurrection save them from beginning to end: "The blood of Jesus, his Son, purifies us from all sin" (v. 7). Christ's sacrifice on the cross continually cleanses his people. Although their performance affects their assurance and enjoyment of God, performance is never the basis for one's relationship with God. Only Christ's saving work occupies that place.

True believers do not live in sin as they would if they did not know Christ. But they never attain sinless perfection in this life. In fact, the longer they walk with Christ, the more they are aware of their sinfulness. John writes, "If we claim to be without sin, we deceive ourselves and the truth is not in us" (v. 8). His words are aimed at the false teachers and their hearers. John directs his message toward a faulty view of sin *and* a defective view of Christ, for a denial of sin implies no need for Christ's saving work. Paul concludes, "If righteousness could be gained through the law, Christ died for nothing!" (Gal. 2:21). Those who deny their sinfulness are self-deceived and shut out God's truth. God is light, and he exposes our sin that we might see our need and come to him for forgiveness and cleansing.

Confession, Forgiveness, and Purification

John gives us one of the most significant verses on the Christian life in Scripture. Instead of denying our sins, true believers acknowledge and confess them to God: "If we confess our sins, he is faithful and just and will forgive us our sins and purify us from all unrighteousness" (v. 9). How can we be confident he will forgive us? We are confident because he is "faithful and just." He is a faithful God, reliable in his character, actions, and words. He is "the faithful God who keeps covenant and steadfast love with those who love him and keep his commandments, to a thousand generations" (Deut. 7:9 ESV). Although Scripture associates God's righteousness with his punishment of sin and sinners (Ps. 96:13; Acts 17:31; Rom. 2:5), astonishingly God's righteousness also brings salvation: "Jesus Christ the righteous is the propitiation for our sins" (1 John 2:2 ESV). As a result of God's faithful and just action in Christ, he forgives and purifies all who sincerely confess their sins.

Universal Sinfulness

John summarizes his rejection of the false teachers' faulty ethic: "If we say we have not sinned, we make him out to be a liar and his word is not in us" (v. 10). John builds on the foundation of other Scripture that underlines the universal sinfulness of fallen human beings:

> There is no one who does not sin. (1 Kings 8:46)

> All have turned away, all have become corrupt;
>> there is no one who does good,
>> not even one. (Ps. 14:3)

> Who can say, "I have kept my heart pure;
>> I am clean and without sin"? (Prov. 20:9)

> Indeed, there is no one on earth who is righteous,
>> no one who does what is right and never sins.
>>> (Eccl. 7:20)

> All have sinned and fall short of the glory of God. (Rom. 3:23)

We all stumble in many ways. (James 3:2)

John points to the shocking conclusion of people claiming to be sinless: it makes God out to be a liar! Yarbrough is correct: "From a first-century Jewish point of view, there could hardly be a greater sacrilege than predicating untruth of God."[9] Paul is emphatic: "Not at all! Let God be true, and every human being a liar" (Rom. 3:4). In fact, those who claim to be without sin show by their claim that God's Word does not dwell in them. What is the God-honoring alternative to the heretics' false theology and ethic? John gives two good answers at the beginning of his next chapter: diligence to avoid sin and recourse to our "advocate with the Father—Jesus Christ, the Righteous One" (1 John 2:1).

CONCLUSION

To understand changed lives and assurance, we must discuss salvation and works. Scripture is clear that although no one will ever be saved by their works, good works flow from God's gift of salvation. Salvation flows from grace and faith in Christ; it is not based on our works. But genuine saving faith "works"—it shows up in believers' changed lives. The same biblical passages that deny salvation by works affirm their importance for authentic Christian living:

> For it is by grace you have been saved, through faith—and this is not from yourselves, it is the gift of God—not by works, so that no one can boast. For we are God's handiwork, created in Christ Jesus to do good works, which God prepared in advance for us to do. (Eph. 2:8–10)

> But when the kindness and love of God our Savior appeared, he saved us, not because of righteous things we had done, but because of his mercy. . . . And I want you to stress these things, so that those who have trusted in God may be careful

> to devote themselves to doing what is good. (Titus 3:4–5, 8;
> cf. Gal. 2:16; 6:9–10)

Changed lives play a role in assurance, but we must nuance this role to avoid misunderstanding. We have studied passages on the importance of changed lives from four biblical authors: Matthew, Paul, Peter, and John. Now, let's pull together several threads of their teaching.

Salvation Makes a Difference in People's Lives

Jesus makes this explicit in the preceding context of Matthew 7:21–23, a passage we studied. Twice he says, "By their fruit you will recognize them" (vv. 16, 20). Although he applies this principle first to false prophets, he broadens it to distinguish believers from unbelievers: "Likewise, every good tree bears good fruit, but a bad tree bears bad fruit. A good tree cannot bear bad fruit, and a bad tree cannot bear good fruit. Every tree that does not bear good fruit is cut down and thrown into the fire" (vv. 17–19). There is a correspondence between what people believe and how they live.

Those who believe in Christ "enter through the narrow gate" that leads to eternal life (vv. 13, 14); they live godly lives. Those who follow "the road that leads to destruction" do not live godly lives (v. 13). This is not to say that the godly never sin, nor that the lost never do good. But the tenor of their lives, the "motion picture" of their life, reveals whether they are saved or lost. Eternal life begins now and shows up in people's lives. That is why 1 John offers comfort to those who evidence eternal life by continuing in faith, love, and holiness. And that is why, even if unbelievers do miracles in Jesus's name, he will "tell them plainly, 'I never knew you. Away from me, you evildoers!'" (v. 23).

Because salvation makes a difference in people's lives, it plays a role in our assurance. It does not occupy pride of place, for that role belongs to God's promises of salvation and preservation. The Word is primary in assurance, but both the Spirit's internal witness and changed lives play vital subordinate roles. We don't base our salvation and assurance on God's working in our lives. But he does work in the lives of his people, and that work reinforces the confidence of salvation that the promise offers.

The Lost Are Recognizable

Passages that we studied teach that unsaved persons' lives reveal their identity. Those who fail to do the Father's will, whom Jesus calls "evildoers" (Matt. 7:23), will not enter the kingdom of heaven (v. 21). "The acts of the flesh are obvious," Paul says, and moreover, "I warn you, as I did before, that those who live like this will not inherit the kingdom of God" (Gal. 5:21).

Because God is perfect holy light, those who walk in the darkness of evil, belie their profession of faith (1 John 1:6). Those who deny sin are self-deceived, contradict the truth of his Word, and in effect call him a "liar" (v. 10). They are certainly not God's children.

Unsaved persons have no right to assurance of salvation. They might have a false sense of assurance, but believers should pray that God would remove unbelievers' false assurance and reveal their need for the Savior.

The Saved Are Recognizable

Only those doing the will of the Father enter the kingdom (Matt. 7:21). God wills that we believe in his Son, love God wholeheartedly, and love our neighbors as ourselves. Union with Christ extends to union in his death and curbs our evil desires (Gal. 5:24). Believers "walk by the Spirit" (vv. 16, 25) and so produce "the fruit of the Spirit" (vv. 22–23).

Christians do not walk in the darkness but in the light. In the light, Jesus's atoning death purifies them from sin (1 John 1:7). They confirm their calling and election by adding Christian virtues to faith. Doing so makes them effective and productive, keeps them from stumbling, and will usher them into God's kingdom (2 Peter 1:5–11). It bears repeating—changed lives play a secondary role in assurance to God's Word.

The Saved Still Must Deal with Sin

Christians are genuinely new but not totally new. Though their lives are not typified by sin, they still commit acts of sin. While the motion picture of their lives shows a Godward bent, they still have embarrassing snapshots. In fact, they are now more aware of their sin than before. They do not deny their sins but confess them to God, who forgives and purifies his people (1 John 1:9).

Walking in the Spirit and in the light involves cultivating humility in dealing with others. Such a spirit could help people like Christine Rosen, whom we met in chapter 1 (p. 21). She would not have left with such a bad taste in her mouth concerning Christianity if her teacher had shown humility instead of giving easy answers to hard questions and belittling others' views. In fact, walking in the Spirit and the light requires sensitivity to our sins and their confession. Paul teaches that because believers have the Spirit, they groan as they wait for final salvation (Rom. 8:23). Ironically, God may use even our confession as evidence of his work in our lives, which can strengthen our assurance.

Furthermore, believers help each other when they sin. As Paul says, "Brothers and sisters, if someone is caught in a sin, you who live by the Spirit should restore that person gently. But watch yourselves, or you also may be tempted. Carry each other's burdens, and in this way you will fulfill the law of Christ" (Gal. 6:1–2). Watching ourselves and helping others are ways God works in us to encourage us. To him be glory!

CHAPTER 8

THE CHURCH AND "DEFENDERS" OF ASSURANCE

In chapter 1 we introduced "troublers," hindrances to believers' assurance of salvation. Now we meet the "defenders" of assurance, the ways God protects and bolsters our assurance. These defenders are found in the church, the primary place God ministers assurance to his people. Before discussing the church and the defenders of assurance, let's review and summarize the means of assurance by looking at Romans 5:1–11.

THE THREE MEANS OF ASSURANCE IN ONE PASSAGE

"A cord of three strands is not quickly broken." (Eccl. 4:12)

God assures believers of final salvation by his Word, Spirit, and work in our lives. Romans 5:1–11 includes all three ways of assurance. God assures us through changing our lives (vv. 3–4), the Spirit's inner witness (v. 5), and the promise of the gospel (vv. 6–11).

157

God's Work

God assures us by working in our lives. We understand what Paul says: "We boast in the hope of the glory of God" (v. 2). By faith we look forward to heaven and resurrection glory. But Paul's next words are difficult: "Not only so, but we also glory in our sufferings" (v. 3). How can this be? Paul explains that it is "because we know that suffering produces perseverance; perseverance, character; and character, hope" (v. 3–4). God uses affliction, rightly handled, to produce endurance. If we keep enduring by his grace, he works in us the character quality of steadfastness. How does becoming steady increase our hope of eternal life? Paul doesn't say, so we must read between the lines. God working in what we can see produces hope for what we cannot see. By witnessing him making us steady, we can hope for unseen heavenly glory.

God's Spirit

Paul states that believers can count on the hope of final salvation. It will not disappoint. Why? "God's love has been poured out into our hearts through the Holy Spirit, who has been given to us" (v. 5). God strengthens our confidence of salvation by his Spirit, who assures us personally, emotionally, and abundantly ("pours out") that God loves us (v. 5). The Spirit testifies deep within that God is our Father and we are his loved children (8:16). We know that we are spiritually united to him, and he to us, because God gave us his Spirit (1 John 3:24; 4:13).

God's Promise

Above all, God assures us by his Word. Paul extols God's staggering love (vv. 6–8) and contrasts God's actions with normal human actions. Rarely will someone give his life for another (v. 7). Such a deed is heroic and always done for someone highly esteemed. A soldier may fall on a grenade for his friends, but never for his foes! But God's love far exceeds human love: "But God demonstrates his own love for us in this: While we were still sinners, Christ died for us" (v. 8). We can never merit God's love. He did not send his Son to die for us because we deserved it. On the contrary, we were "powerless," "ungodly," "sinners" (vv. 6, 8) when Christ gave himself for us.

After exalting God's love that assures future glory, Paul says God keeps to the end those he has saved. Twice Paul uses "how much more" to argue from the harder to the easier, first on justification (v. 9) and then on reconciliation (v. 10). If God did the harder thing and justified condemned sinners, he will certainly do the easier one and preserve those he has justified till the end. The apostle increases confidence of final salvation. God did the inconceivable thing and pronounced unrighteous sinners righteous in Christ. Now he will do the expected thing: honor his earlier verdict and not condemn his justified people.

To underscore his point, Paul makes a similar argument for preservation. This time he speaks of reconciliation instead of justification. "For if, while we were God's enemies, we were reconciled to him through the death of his Son, how much more, having been reconciled, shall we be saved through his life!" (Rom. 5:10). If through his Son's death God made us his friends when we were his foes, now that we are his friends, he surely will sustain us for final salvation through his Son's resurrection.

Paul thus praises the unimaginable love of God, who gave his Son to deliver sinners. He returns to the idea of hope and accentuates its certainty. Twice Paul says unambiguously that we shall be saved (vv. 9, 10). Our heavenly Father loves us and wants us to have confidence in his promises that guarantee our final salvation in Christ. The most powerful basis for assurance is God's Word, the gospel, the promise of salvation.

Speaking of Romans 5:9–10, Judith Gundry Volf hits the nail on the head:

> Paul draws out the significance of God's gracious love as
> the guarantee that Christian hope will not disappoint. . . .
> With the help of two arguments . . . he shows that God's

accomplishment of the scarcely imaginable feat of demonstrating love toward rebellious sinners in the cross of Christ guarantees the future salvation of those who are God's own people in fulfillment of their hope.[1]

THE CHURCH: THE LOCATION OF GOD'S DEFENDERS OF ASSURANCE

It's a mistake to consider gaining assurance to be a self-help program. We do not manufacture assurance. God graciously gives assurance. God also never intended us to live the Christian life alone. When God joined us to Christ, he joined us to others joined to Christ. God strengthens assurance in and by his church.

Throughout this book we have affirmed that God assures us by his Word, Spirit, and work in our lives. It's time to see how God applies these means of assurance in the church. God's ministries of Word, Spirit, and believers are "defenders" of assurance that strengthen our confidence that we belong to the Lord.

These defenders of assurance are:

- The ministries of God's Word
- The ministries of God's Spirit
- The ministries of God's people

The Ministries of God's Word
The Church Is the Body of Christ

The ministries of God's Word, which are the chief defenders of assurance, are located in the body of Christ. As the head of the body, Christ is the church's authority and the source of its spiritual life (Col. 1:18, 2:19). Christ is the head, and we are the members, the body parts (1 Cor. 12:27). The chief role of the Holy Spirit in salvation is to join believers to Christ and to one another in one body (v. 13).

The image of the body conveys the relationship of believers to Christ, the members to their head (Rom. 12:6–8). Just as our bodily members belong to us, so believers belong to Christ. And by virtue of union with Christ, the members belong to each other (1 Cor. 12:14–27).

God entrusts the work of Christ's church to Christ and his people. Church leaders should train members to engage in ministry to edify Christ's body (Eph. 4:12). Christ provides the stimulus for growth, but both the head and its members are active in bodily growth (vv. 15–16). The body image is dynamic, for the body grows and matures (v. 13).

Chiefly, God works through the gospel as it is preached, taught in Sunday school, and communicated in baptism and the Lord's Supper. He strengthens the faith of his servants as they minister his Word. All these ministries of the Word, which are primarily located in the church, are defenders of assurance.

Sermons

God commands his ministers to "preach the Word" (2 Tim. 4:2) and believers humbly to accept the Word that saves them (James 1:21). God uses his Word, whether preached or taught, to build us up in our faith.

God drew me to himself as a twenty-one-year-old. On summer break from college, I worked in a tire factory, where a godly man encouraged me to read the Bible. I did and soon found myself devouring the Word. I heard sound sermons at a Bible-believing church and attended Sunday school, where Scripture was faithfully taught. As a result I came to know Christ and gained a great sense of assurance, which I could not explain. God was merciful to me and used his Word to save me and give me confidence that I belonged to him. By his grace his Word has continued to be my source of hope and life (Ps. 119:49–50).

Sunday School

Sunday school is a time of special teaching beyond the sermon. It is practiced in various ways today, not always under the name "Sunday school." God calls people to be students of the

Word, like the Bereans who "examined the Scriptures" to confirm what Paul told them was true (Acts 17:11).

A pastor once shared this true story with me:

> A man named John in our church struggled for years with guilt and assurance of salvation. He would regularly go into his cold garage in the winter wearing little clothing, get on his knees on the cold floor, and beg God to forgive him. He sometimes did this for several hours at a time but never felt truly at peace with God. I was teaching through the book of Romans in an adult Sunday school class and came to justification by faith alone from Romans 3:21–4:8. John looked up from his open Bible with a look of amazement. He had tears in his eyes. He later told me about his ongoing struggles with assurance of salvation and his long-endured sense of alienation from God. He said that as he heard these passages and teaching on them, he understood the gospel more fully and knew he was truly forgiven and accepted by God. His Christian life dramatically changed that day. As he understood and believed the gospel, God assured him of salvation.

Baptism and the Lord's Supper

Baptism and the Lord's Supper do not always receive the attention they deserve. As ceremonial presentations of the gospel, they play roles in assurance. In many respects, the church's two ordinances are dissimilar. Baptism is the initial rite of the Christian faith, and the Lord's Supper is its ongoing rite. Their material elements differ, for baptism involves water while the Supper involves bread and the fruit of the vine. Paul taught that baptism is to be performed only once: "There is one . . . baptism" (Eph. 4:4–5). By contrast, he also taught that the Lord's Supper is to be observed repeatedly: "whenever you eat this bread and drink this cup . . . until he comes" (1 Cor. 11:26).

Baptism and the Lord's Supper also have similarities. Christ instituted both ordinances at his command (Matt. 26:26–29;

28:18–20). Both play important roles in the Christian life. Although Paul assigns several meanings to each, he teaches that the most basic and profound meaning of both is union with Christ. This is true for Christian baptism, which depicts initial union with Christ (Rom. 6:1–14; Gal. 3:25–28; Col. 2:11–12), and for the Lord's Supper, which depicts ongoing union with Christ (1 Cor. 10:16–17; 11:23–26).

Neither baptism nor the Lord's Supper bears new content, but both tell the "old, old story of Jesus and his love." That is, both portray the gospel in a ceremony. Jesus was very gracious to his church. He not only commanded pastors to "preach the word" (2 Tim. 4:2); he also built the Word into the church's two basic ceremonies. We see this in Augustine's and Calvin's idea that baptism and communion are "visible words."[2] They are visual depictions of the gospel.

As often as the church observes the Lord's Supper, "you *proclaim* the Lord's death until he comes" (1 Cor. 11:26). The Lord's Supper and its words of institution proclaim the gospel. The same is true for baptism, which is done with water, a universal cleansing agent, and carries the promise of the forgiveness of sins (Acts 2:38–39). Baptism is a means of grace in our lives that strengthens our faith. Witnessing the baptism of others can often be a source of encouragement and reassurance. Likewise, the Lord's Supper is a defender of assurance. Jesus instituted it so Christians would never forget his death and resurrection. Like baptism, the Lord's Supper declares the gospel.[3]

My friend Jim shares his testimony:

I was raised in a Christian home. My parents gave me a big, red-letter KJV Bible on my sixth birthday, which I faithfully carried to Sunday school each week. In the church-sponsored scouting program, I weekly pledged "to do my duty to God and country, and to keep myself morally straight." The result of this training in Scouts and at home: I came to believe that if I was good, God would be pleased with me. In church,

I heard "God so loved the world that he gave his only begotten Son," and I concluded that I believe God sent his Son, so I must be okay with God.

In mid-July 1967, a few weeks prior to my seventeenth birthday, I attended a weeklong Christian Youth Conference at Berry College in Rome, Georgia. On the final evening, we broke into groups of about ten to receive the Lord's Supper. As the pastor for my group served the elements, he emphasized the last word in his statement to each of us: "the body of Christ, given for *you*; the blood of Christ, shed for *you*." When I heard those words, Jesus's sacrificial death suddenly became specific to me, Jim, rather than being only a general gift to the whole world. Instantly I was changed, new, clean, and deeply loved. In my mind's eye the image persisted for a week of me embracing the ankles of my Lord and not wanting to move from that spot. Though I have struggled at times in the years since, that event marked the beginning of my journey of knowing, loving, and serving Jesus, who loved me and gave himself for me, who loves me still and keeps me. Of course, the Lord's Supper continues to mean a great deal to me.

Ministry of the Word

God blesses those who minister the Word (Acts 20:32). He enables them to help others and helps them as they do. Today Dan, a veteran missionary and educator, enjoys confidence in Christ. It was not always so, as he explains:

As a young missionary, I was struggling with my calling and even my identity in Christ. My wife and I were visiting a crowded Asian city. I had been asked to teach a series from the book of Daniel at an evening chapel for a small Bible institute. I had prepared my notes but was not very excited about the long trip through the city, and I wasn't sure how my teaching would be received.

On the way to the meeting, traffic was terrible. I felt a

migraine beginning. When we arrived at the Bible Institute, there was an electrical "brownout." Things were not going well. Or so I thought.

When the time came for me to teach, a pastor placed candles near each student. A young man held a flashlight, so I could see my notes and write on the blackboard. As I began to teach God's Word and looked into the students' eager faces, the truth of Holy Scripture began to convict me. God's Spirit wisely used this teaching experience to increase my courage and confidence.

Since that day many years ago, whenever I sense discouragement or a wandering heart, I find a way to share or teach God's Word. I've learned that serving others in the ministry of the Word can be a significant source of assurance.

The Ministries of God's Spirit
The Church Is the Temple of the Spirit

The church is the Spirit's special dwelling place, where he bolsters and defends assurance. Peter presents the church as a living temple with Christ as the "living Stone," alive from death (1 Peter 2:4). Believers in Christ are "living stones . . . being built into a spiritual house" (vv. 4–5). Christ gives his people spiritual life. The church is an organism, alive with Jesus's resurrection life. Through union with him "he has given us new birth into a living hope" (1:3), and together we form the church, a living temple where God is worshiped.

Against the background of Solomon's magnificent temple, Paul boldly calls Christians "God's temple" (1 Cor. 3:16, 17). Paul teaches that the Spirit occupies the place that a god or goddess would in a Greco-Roman temple. In fact, in Paul's passages treating the church as a temple (1 Cor. 3:16–17; 6:19–20; 2 Cor. 6:16; Eph. 2:19–22), he says it is God's presence that makes a church a church. Paul presents this temple of God's people as dynamic and organic, a building growing into a temple before our eyes (Eph. 2:21–22). Paul says that God forms this temple to promote

Trinitarian worship: "Through [Christ] we both have access to the Father by one Spirit" (Eph. 2:18).

Peter and Paul portray God's people as a temple, a living sanctuary where the Trinity is worshiped. God uses defenders of assurance, what takes place in this temple, to strengthen his people's confidence of salvation.

Public Worship

Corporate worship characterized the early church (Acts 13:12; Eph. 5:18–20; Col. 3:16). The Spirit enabled and facilitated worship then and continues to do so today. In the public worship of God today, believers gather to praise, pray, confess their sins, return to God a fraction of his bounty, affirm their faith, observe baptism and the Lord's Supper, and receive the preached Word of God. Scripture directs the church to do these things. Why? The most important reasons have to do with God and his glory. But God also directs us in public worship for our good.

God builds us up in holy faith and confirms his love for and hold on us as we worship him with like-minded believers. In chapter 1 (pp. 18–19) we met Ruth Tucker, a woman who perseveres in her faith despite lingering doubts. When she is asked what keeps her going, she answers:

> This is my culture, my tradition. I love the Bible stories and the old hymns of the faith. I can close my eyes and see Jesus "on a hill far away on that old rugged cross." I love to sit at the piano and sing "Softly and Tenderly Jesus Is Calling" and the other invitation hymns in the pages that follow in that tattered hymnbook. I teach my darling granddaughter Kayla songs and Bible verses. This is my faith, and I will never abandon it—nor will God abandon me.[4]

Our focus in worship is rightly on God. Yet God graciously uses our worship of him as a way to strengthen our confidence of salvation. Worship is thus another defender of assurance.

Encouragement

The early church exercised a ministry of encouragement (1 Thess. 5:11, 14). Such a ministry continues today. I remember the first time Karl and Linda joined the small group that meets in our home. They were so discouraged that if they had been canines, their tails would have been between their legs! When they were offered an opportunity to speak, they shared how they feared we would not want such troubled people in our group! Their children were not living for the Lord, so Karl and Linda condemned themselves as unfaithful parents.

I will never forget the immediate responses of our small group members and the effect on our visitors. "You've come to the right group, friends!" one woman said. A man added, "We are thankful that our kids take turns getting into trouble, so we can lift each other up. If all our kids hit bottom at once, we would all fall into despair!"

Quickly our new friends saw that no one in the group judged them. Instead, we all struggled and found help in sharing with the others. As was our custom, we lifted up one another, including Karl and Linda, during prayer time. Once more, they saw no condescension but genuine empathy and prayers to God on their behalf. In time we watched God encourage and build them up. They gained confidence in the Lord and helped others in the group as well.

Love

Both Testaments commend the marvelous love of God (Ps. 103:11; Eph. 3:14–19). Paul exalts love above faith and hope (1 Cor. 13:13). Jesus and his apostles insist that God's people show love (John 13:34; 1 John 3:16–17). Human love is powerful, and sadly, I have heard of people being drawn by love into unorthodox offshoots of Christianity that deny the essentials of the faith. Thankfully, God's love is more powerful. I have a friend Katherine, whom God delivered out of Christian Science. She tells her story:

I grew up a third-generation Christian Scientist living on the St. Louis campus of their Principia School, which I attended through my first year of college. I left Christian Science after September 11, 2001, when I was saw the undeniable reality of evil in the world. Confused by the inconsistencies between Christian Science and the world, I lived in spiritual darkness for the next seven years. In 2008 I overheard a conversation on faith in a coffee shop that gave me hope. I desired to know God and was convicted of my sinful heart, so I read Francis Schaeffer's *The God Who Is There.*

I began attending Grace and Peace Fellowship in St. Louis, where I first experienced the gospel, seeing the love of the body of Christ in action. I wept throughout the entire first service, and I think I believed immediately. The pastor preached a sermon on biblical love in marriage in a way I had never heard before. I was completely drawn in and never looked back. Pastor Turner kindly and patiently spent countless hours studying Scripture with me and walked with me to faith. My eyes were opened to see what the Bible actually said rather than what Mary Baker Eddy taught. The church was extremely loving toward me. There I came to know the God of Scripture and professed Jesus as my Savior. I was baptized just two months later, went to seminary, and graduated in 2013.

I met another former Christian Scientist, and connecting with her was incredibly helpful and healing. Hearing her story helped me understand mine better. I felt called to reach out to other former Christian Scientists. I realized there was a real need for a ministry working to connect former Christian Scientists and provide resources specifically for them. I found others were praying for this too. This led me to form Fellowship of Former Christian Scientists in January of 2014.

God used his Word and Christians' love to draw Katherine to himself. The gospel ministered in love overcame her obstacles to faith and gave her assurance of God's love.

The Ministries of God's People

The Church Is the People of God

The people of God began with Adam and Eve in Eden. Later, God called Abraham and promised to make from him a great nation to bless all families on earth. God called Israel out of Egyptian bondage to be his people and gave them the promised land and later David as king in Jerusalem. When Israel continually rejected God's prophets, he sent them into captivity. He sent more prophets who promised that God would restore Israel to their land, which God accomplished.

After four hundred years God sent his Son as promised Messiah, King of Israel, and Savior of the world. Jesus chose disciples and after his death and resurrection sent them to take the gospel to all nations to fulfill his promise to Abraham. Christ sent his Spirit, who constituted the church as the New Testament people of God. Peter described the churches to which he wrote with Old Testament language originally addressed to Israel (1 Peter 2:9–10). The church as the people of God is spiritual Israel (cf. Gal. 6:16; Phil. 3:3).

The church is "those who have been called, who are loved in God the Father and kept for Jesus Christ" (Jude 1). The people of God belong to him, and amazingly, he belongs to them (Rev. 21:3). God strengthens his people, the church, as they minister in various ways.

Fellowship (Small Groups)

"Our fellowship is with the Father and with his Son, Jesus Christ" (1 John 1:3). One of the best places for Christians to minister to each other is fellowship groups, cell groups, or small groups. At their healthiest, small groups are characterized by Bible study, prayer, and sharing. John Stott rejoices in the worldwide spread of small groups today: "One of the most encouraging features of the world Christian scene today has been the recovery of small groups."[5] Moreover, he regards small groups as indispensable to Christian maturity: "I do not think it is an exaggeration to say, therefore, that small groups, Christian family or fellowship groups, are indispensable for our growth into spiritual maturity."[6]

I have heard more than one pastor credit small groups as places where Christians listen to and serve one another. I already spoke of God's using our home group to encourage and strengthen its members. Over time, we have seen God use the ministries of his Word, prayer, and fellowship to build up new believers in their faith. It is a joy to see them grow and develop a desire to help others. We have thus seen God use the small group as a defender of assurance.

Evangelism

Often believers find their faith strengthened when sharing the gospel with unbelievers. Although they intend to minister to the person they seek to lead to Christ (1 Thess. 1:8), God works in their hearts as well. Tom's story is one of failure to win his father but unintended successful increase of his confidence in Christ.

Tom is a Christian man who has walked with the Lord for many years. He is active in his church and enjoys friendships with both believers and unbelievers. While his father was still alive, Tom frequently talked to him about Christianity with no success. His father was a brilliant man with a very high IQ. He was a scientist and a militant atheist. Their conversations were lengthy, animated, and respectful. Tom's father raised many questions that Tom could not answer. These questions drove him to do research to answer various objections that his father raised. Sadly, despite Tom's prayers and evangelistic efforts, his father died in unbelief. Tom grieved the loss of his dad but received an unexpected benefit. He was surprised to realize that his interactions with his father, in answering his objections, had strengthened his own faith.

Prayer

If you believe, you will receive whatever you ask for in prayer. (Matt. 21:22)

Devote yourselves to prayer, being watchful and thankful. (Col. 4:2)

God ministers to his people in numerous ways when they pray for each other. He invigorates their spiritual lives. He motivates them to praise, confession, and thanksgiving. He increases their faith by answering their prayers and lets them see his answers to their prayers help others.

Such was the case with Barb, whose testimony has helped many going through serious illness. At fifteen, Barb was diagnosed with terminal ovarian cancer. Her medical records showed that it had spread to two lymph nodes. She was not a Christian at the time. After sixteen weeks of radiation therapy, her cancer went into remission and the tumors disappeared. God deserves the glory, but he used the prayers of many believers.

Barb is quick to remind others that God does not always answer prayers for healing. About ten years later she became a Christian, and this too came after years of faithful believers' prayers. Her pastor thanks God for sparing Barb. She is now fifty-seven, loves the Lord, and ministers to others in many ways. She teaches a children's Sunday school class, leads a youth group with her husband, and coleads a women's Bible study.

In answer to prayer God healed and saved Barb so that, in the words of her pastor's wife, "she has been a blessing to all who know her."

Missions Trips

God uses mission trips to help those who go to minister as well as those whom they serve, as Diane's story bears witness:

A missionary requested that a team from our evangelical church accompany him to Lebanon to see a ministry to the Syrian refugee camps along the Syria-Lebanon border. As a member of the church's mission committee, I thought this request was too late because it was April and our church plans mission trips a year in advance. The committee prayed and talked to church leaders, two of whom agreed to go to evaluate how our church could possibly serve this ministry in the future. Although I was not planning to go, they asked me to accompany them. As a woman, I was anxious about what to expect in Lebanon and had some reservations about my safety. I talked to God about it, and knew that whatever might be ahead of me, dangers or not, he would be with me. So I joined them.

If I had given in to my fears, I would have missed one of the most amazing experiences of my life. We had heard of Syrians coming to Christ, but we saw and heard this with our own eyes and ears. We saw amazing ministries: a Christian school in a tent, a church half-filled with Muslims (some of whom were new believers), and a women's weekly Bible study in the tent community.

We were invited to visit three families the missionaries have been discipling. In each tent, we were humbly served from their meager stores as if we were kings and queens and asked to share the gospel with them. As God gave us words to share, translated into Arabic, God opened my eyes to see what he is doing in the world. How could I have doubted?

Discipline

"If someone is caught in a sin, you who live by the Spirit should restore that person gently. But watch yourselves, or you also may be tempted" (Gal. 6:1). John Calvin taught that there were three main purposes for church discipline: God's glory, the reclamation of the repentant sinner, and warning to the church.

The following story highlights the first two purposes because the matter was kept confidential. Joan, a member of a Baptist church, noticed a man from her church at a restaurant with a woman who was not his wife. It looked like more than a meeting of friends. Joan told a church officer, who in turn spoke to the pastor. The two church leaders met with the man and asked him about it, and he confessed that he was unhappy at home and was starting to see this woman. He said they had not yet had a sexual relationship but were moving in that direction. Church discipline takes many forms, from gentle rebuke to excommunication from the Lord's Supper. In this case discipline took the form of a strong and loving warning. The leaders warned the man that pursuing that adulterous relationship was inconsistent with his profession of Christ.

He responded to the warning and broke off the relationship. He and his wife sought counseling, which helped them, and they remained married for the rest of their lives. Both the man and his wife were brought closer to Christ because of the church leaders' care and the man's positive response to discipline. It does not surprise us to learn that the man's assurance was at a low ebb when he contemplated adultery. It also should not surprise us that when he turned from sin and obeyed Christ, he became more confident in his relationship to God. God used discipline to defend a marriage and a man's salvation and assurance.

Service

> Serve one another humbly in love. (Gal. 5:13)

> Let us do good to all people, especially to those who belong to the family of believers. (Gal. 6:10)

God calls us to serve him, other believers, and those outside of the family of God. He uses our service to minister to others and to build up their confidence in Christ. Sometimes when we least expect it, God uses our service of others to strengthen us, as Donna's story shows:

> As mission leader, who led many short-term missions' teams, I find that God surprises me every time I follow him in this way. This year was no exception. I hadn't planned to be on any short-term mission teams but intended to allow others

to go. The Lord had other plans. Our church received an invitation from a veteran missionary who had never invited a short-term team. Two years ago, God led him to leave a liberal denomination and plant a biblical church. We wondered whether going was a waste of time and our supporters' money. We couldn't imagine what God had in mind. Nevertheless, we went to serve his church and show love by caring for infants and toddlers at a church family camp. The first day was impossibly hard. Our foreign language scared the toddlers, the stuffy room was 100 degrees, and opening the door for air invited toddlers to escape. But we prayed, and God answered. The week went smoothly, and we began to bond with the children and their parents. Then we were asked to be guest speakers for an evening program at the camp about what church community at our home church looked like. Though we didn't know it at the time, God used us and what we shared to break down barriers of tradition that were holding the church back from experiencing what God had for them. Not only did barriers fall (they had never experienced small group Bible studies or Sunday school before, and now began to desire both), but two adults trusted Christ. I left ashamed. I had wondered why God was wasting our time and talent, but his way was perfect. I rejoice that in using me God encouraged me in my faith.

🌲 🌲 🌲

Believers will never completely lose the "troublers" of assurance in this life, whether in their own experience or the experience of those they care about. Thankfully, the Lord wants us to have assurance, and he has provided "defenders" to encourage us. The defenders follow from the three ways God assures us. How good of God not only to save us but to build up our confidence of salvation through Scripture, the Holy Spirit, and working in our lives! We sing with the psalmist:

Praise him for his acts of power;
    praise him for his surpassing greatness. (Ps. 150:2)

In God's wisdom he incorporated these three means of assurance into the life of the church. The Word, the Spirit, and believers are God's defenders against the troublers.

It remains for us to get involved in some of these ministries as God gives us gifts and opportunity. We can encourage others to do the same. As we apply ourselves to serve God, other believers, and lost people, God will use us to help some, and he will build us up in our holy faith. May our gracious God encourage strugglers (all of us at times!) to take as full a measure of assurance as we can from him.

Praise be to his holy name!

ACKNOWLEDGMENTS

I am grateful to those who helped me on this project: Mary Pat, for her love, faithfulness, and prayers; my friends at Zondervan, Katya Covrett and Stan Gundry, for believing in, supporting, and encouraging me when I needed it most; my friends at Costco in Manchester, MO, including manager Rob, for providing me with space to write and walk; my friends at Valenti's Delicatessen in St. Charles, MO, for kindly hosting me as I worked on this manuscript, especially Rachael, Kathy, and Lindsey; my friends at Town Square Pub N Grub in Dardenne Prairie, MO, for friendship and inspiration; Pastor Russ St. John and the brothers and sisters of Twin Oaks Presbyterian Church, Twin Oaks, Missouri, for their prayers, especially the flock of Dave and Diane Bruegger; and Christopher Morgan, for taking time to read the manuscript and offer comments. Special thanks are due to my editor extraordinaire, Matthew Estel, for patience, expertise, and great encouragement; Daniel Ebert IV, for painstakingly working through the manuscript and giving me much help; Pastor Van Lees, for his friendship and prayers; and Elliott Pinegar, for skillful and timely help with abstruse editorial questions.

NOTES

Introduction

1. For the sake of privacy, facts (names, details) in these personal stories have been changed.
2. Jon Tal Murphree, *Security in Christ: Does "Once Saved" Mean "Always Saved"?* (University Park, IA: Vennard College, 2002), 10, 13, 78.
3. *Catechism of the Catholic Church* (New York: Doubleday, 1995), para. 157 (p. 48) and para. 161–62 (p. 50).
4. J. I. Packer, *Knowing God* (Downers Grove, IL: InterVarsity Press, 1973), 189, 237–38, emphasis original.
5. D. A. Carson, "Reflections on Assurance," in *Still Sovereign: Contemporary Perspectives on Election, Foreknowledge, and Grace,* ed. Thomas R. Schreiner and Bruce A. Ware (Grand Rapids: Baker, 2000), 274–75.

Chapter 1: "Troublers" of Assurance

1. I thank Brian Aucker, associate professor of Old Testament at Covenant Theological Seminary, for this definition.
2. Ruth Tucker, *Walking Away from Faith: Unraveling the Mystery of Belief and Unbelief* (Downers Grove, IL: InterVarsity Press, 2002).
3. Tucker, *Walking Away from Faith*, 26.
4. Tucker, *Walking Away from Faith*, 27.
5. Tucker, *Walking Away from Faith*, 27, emphasis original.
6. Tucker, *Walking Away from Faith*, 26.
7. Christine Wicker, *God Knows My Heart: Finding a Faith that Fits* (New York: St. Martin's, 1999), as referenced by Scot McKnight and Hauna Ondrey, *Finding Faith, Losing Faith: Stories of Conversion and Apostasy* (Waco, TX: Baylor University Press, 2008), 10.
8. McKnight and Ondrey, *Finding Faith, Losing Faith*, 10.

9. McKnight and Ondrey, *Finding Faith, Losing Faith*, 10.

10. McKnight and Ondrey, *Finding Faith, Losing Faith*, 12.

11. McKnight and Ondrey, *Finding Faith, Losing Faith*, 27.

12. C. John Collins, *Science and Faith: Friends or Foes?* (Wheaton, IL: Crossway, 2003); Collins, *Did Adam and Eve Really Exist? Who They Were and Why You Should Care* (Wheaton, IL: Crossway, 2011); Bernard Ramm, *The Christian View of Science and Scripture* (Grand Rapids: Eerdmans, 1954); Michael J. Behe, *Darwin's Black Box: The Biochemical Challenge to Evolution* (New York: Free Press, 1996); J. P. Moreland and John Mark Reynolds, eds., *Three Views on Creation and Evolution* (Grand Rapids: Zondervan, 1999); J. P. Moreland, ed., *The Creation Hypothesis* (Downers Grove, IL: InterVarsity Press, 1994); Michael Denton, *Evolution: A Theory in Crisis* (Bethesda, MD: Adler & Adler, 1986); William A. Dembski, *Intelligent Design: The Bridge Between Science and Theology* (Downers Grove, IL: Intervarsity Press, 1999).

13. McKnight and Ondrey, *Finding Faith, Losing Faith*, 22.

14. McKnight and Ondrey, *Finding Faith, Losing Faith*, 22.

15. Tucker, *Walking Away from Faith*, 107. The Dawkins quotation is from Alvin Plantinga, "Darwin, Mind and Meaning," *Books and Culture* (May-June 1996): 35.

16. Os Guinness, *God in the Dark: The Assurance of Faith Beyond a Shadow of Doubt* (Wheaton, IL: Crossway, 1996), 129–30.

17. Guinness, *God in the Dark*, 130.

18. McKnight and Ondrey, *Finding Faith, Losing Faith*, 27–28.

19. Phil Zuckerman, *Faith No More: Why People Reject Religion* (New York: Oxford University Press, 2012), 88.

20. McKnight and Ondrey, *Finding Faith, Losing Faith*, 28.

21. Zuckerman, *Faith No More*, 89.

22. McKnight and Ondrey, *Finding Faith, Losing Faith*, 29.

23. Tucker, *Walking Away from Faith*, 185–86.

24. Tucker, *Walking Away from Faith*, 189.

25. Tucker, *Walking Away from Faith*, 184, 186.

26. Tullian Tchividjian, *Do I Know God? Finding Certainty in Life's Most Important Relationships* (Colorado Springs: Multnomah, 2007), 42.

Chapter 2: Assurance and the Gospel

1. Anthony A. Hoekema, *Saved by Grace* (Grand Rapids: Eerdmans, 1989), 70–72.

2. F. F. Bruce, *The Gospel of John* (Grand Rapids: Eerdmans, 1983), 91.

3. D. A. Carson, *The Gospel according to John*, Pillar New Testament Commentaries (Grand Rapids: Eerdmans, 1991), 206.

4. Leon Morris, *The Gospel according to John*, New International

Commentary on the New Testament (Grand Rapids: Eerdmans, 1971), 316.

5. Carson, *The Gospel according to John*, 256.
6. Frank Thielman, *Ephesians*, Baker Exegetical Commentary on the New Testament (Grand Rapids: Baker Academic, 2010), 135.
7. F. F. Bruce, *The Epistles to the Colossians, to Philemon, and to the Ephesians*, New International Commentary on the New Testament (Grand Rapids: Eerdmans, 1984), 287.
8. William L. Lane, *Hebrews 1–8*, Word Biblical Commentary (Dallas: Word, 1991), 189. The Greek is *eis to panteles*.
9. F. F. Bruce, *The Epistle to the Hebrews*, New International Commentary on the New Testament (Grand Rapids: Eerdmans, 1964), 155.
10. Philip Edgcumbe Hughes, *A Commentary on the Epistle to the Hebrews* (Grand Rapids: Eerdmans, 1977), 269–70.
11. Bruce, *The Epistle to the Hebrews*, 241.
12. Wayne Grudem, *1 Peter*, Tyndale New Testament Commentaries (Grand Rapids: Eerdmans, 1988), 58.
13. Thomas R. Schreiner, *1, 2 Peter, Jude*, New American Commentary (Nashville: B&H, 2003), 63.
14. Peter H. Davids, *The First Epistle of Peter*, New International Commentary on the New Testament (Grand Rapids: Eerdmans, 1990), 53.
15. Schreiner, *1, 2 Peter, Jude*, 64, 65.

Chapter 3: Assurance and Preservation in John

1. This follows from my work in *Our Secure Salvation: Preservation and Apostasy*, Explorations in Biblical Theology (Phillipsburg, NJ: P&R, 2009).
2. Robert W. Yarbrough, *1–3 John*, Baker Exegetical Commentary on the New Testament (Grand Rapids: Baker Academic, 2008), 146–47, emphasis original.
3. John R. W. Stott, *The Letters of John*, rev. ed., Tyndale New Testament Commentaries (Grand Rapids: Eerdmans, 1964; repr., 1988), 111.
4. John's use of the second-class condition here is important. Daniel Wallace, a recognized linguist, says that such a Greek conditional sentence "indicates *the assumption of an untruth (for the sake of argument)*" and includes 1 John 2:19 in this category. Daniel B. Wallace, *Greek Grammar beyond the Basics: An Exegetical Syntax of the New Testament* (Grand Rapids: Zondervan, 1996), 694, 696, emphasis original.
5. D. E. Hiebert, "An Exposition of 1 John 2:18–28," *Bibliotheca Sacra* (1989): 81, as reported in Daniel L. Akin, *1, 2, 3 John*, New American Commentary (Nashville: B&H, 2001), 116.

6. D. A. Carson, "Reflections on Assurance," in *Still Sovereign*, ed. Thomas R. Schreiner and Bruce A. Ware (Grand Rapids: Baker, 2000), 264.

7. St. Augustine, "On the Gift of Perseverance," in *Nicene and Post-Nicene Fathers*, ed. Philip Schaff (repr., Grand Rapids: Eerdmans, 1991), 5:532, 538.

8. For evidence for this predominant view, see Stephen S. Smalley, *1, 2, 3 John*, Word Biblical Commentary (Waco, TX: Word, 1984), 303.

9. Smalley, *1, 2, 3 John*, 303. Here, the Greek for *touch* is *haptetai*. Cf. Walter Bauer, William F. Arndt, F. Wilbur Gingrich, and Frederick W. Danker, *A Greek-English Lexicon of the New Testament and Other Early Christian Literature*, 2nd ed. (Chicago: University of Chicago Press, 1979), 103.

10. Stott, *The Letters of John*, 195, emphasis original.

11. It also occurs in John 10:29; 17:2, 6, 9, and 24.

12. Thomas R. Schreiner and Ardel B. Caneday, *The Race Set before Us: A Biblical Theology of Perseverance and Assurance* (Downers Grove, IL: InterVarsity Press, 2001), 250.

13. Daniel B. Wallace, *Greek Grammar Beyond the Basics: An Exegetical Syntax of the New Testament* (Grand Rapids: Zondervan, 1996), 468, emphasis original.

14. Wallace, *Greek Grammar Beyond the Basics*, 468, italics original and bold removed.

15. Carson, *The Gospel according to John*, Pillar New Testament Commentary (Grand Rapids: Eerdmans, 1991), 393, emphasis original.

16. Leon Morris, *The Gospel according to John*, New International Commentary on the New Testament (Grand Rapids: Eerdmans, 1971), 521.

17. Though Jesus here uses an imperative to address the Father—"Protect them"—of course he is not commanding him. Imperatives are used in prayers to express requests. See Wallace, *Greek Grammar Beyond the Basics*, 487–88.

18. Carson, *The Gospel according to John*, 562.

19. Grant R. Osborne, "Soteriology in the Gospel of John," in *The Grace of God, the Will of Man*, ed. Clark H. Pinnock (Grand Rapids: Zondervan, 1989), 249, 254.

20. Schreiner and Caneday, *The Race Set before Us*, 253–54.

Chapter 4: Assurance and Preservation in Paul

1. Alister E. McGrath, *The Sunnier Side of Doubt* (Grand Rapids: Zondervan, 1990), 27–28.

2. I received help from my *Our Secure Salvation: Preservation and Apostasy*, Explorations in Biblical Theology (Phillipsburg, NJ: P&R Publishing, 2009).

3. The emphatic negative *ouden* is used and is put first for emphasis.

4. C. E. B. Cranfield, *A Critical and Exegetical Commentary on the Epistle to the Romans*, 2 vols., International Critical Commentary (Edinburgh: T&T Clark, 1975), 1:373.

5. This is because the words "for sin" are used regularly in the Septuagint (the Greek Old Testament) to mean "sin offering," and most commentators interpret them that way here. See James D. G. Dunn, *Romans 1–9*, Word Biblical Commentary (Waco, TX: Word, 1988), 403.

6. Douglas J. Moo, *The Epistle to the Romans*, New International Commentary on the New Testament (Grand Rapids: Eerdmans, 1996), 481.

7. See my *Election and Free Will*, Explorations in Biblical Theology (Phillipsburg, NJ: P&R, 2007).

8. Thomas R. Schreiner, *Romans*, Baker Exegetical Commentary on the New Testament (Grand Rapids: Baker, 1998), 454.

9. Schreiner, *Romans*, 463.

10. Note that seven is sometimes used in Scripture to show completeness.

11. In part 2, we will focus more completely on the inner witness of the Holy Spirit in believers' assurance.

12. Peter T. O'Brien, *The Letter to the Ephesians*, Pillar New Testament Commentary (Grand Rapids: Eerdmans, 1999), 348.

13. Judith M. Gundry Volf, *Paul and Perseverance, Staying In and Falling Away* (Louisville: Westminster John Knox, 1990), 32.

14. Peter T. O'Brien, *The Epistle to the Philippians*, New International Greek Testament Commentary (Grand Rapids: Eerdmans, 1991), 64, emphasis original.

15. O'Brien, *The Epistle to the Philippians*, 65.

16. I was taught this by F. F. Bruce, *1 & 2 Thessalonians*, Word Biblical Commentary (Waco, TX: Word, 1982), 70–71, 128.

17. Gordon D. Fee, *The First and Second Letters to the Thessalonians*, New International Commentary on the New Testament (Grand Rapids: Eerdmans, 2009), 231.

18. Leon Morris, *The First and Second Epistles to the Thessalonians*, New International Commentary on the New Testament (Grand Rapids: Eerdmans, 1959), 182–83.

Chapter 5: The Holy Spirit's Person and Work

1. In this section, I work from and have adapted, elaborated, or simplified information from my *Salvation Applied by the Spirit: Union with Christ* (Wheaton, IL: Crossway, 2014), 295–306.

2. I received help from my *Salvation Applied by the Spirit*, 307–47.

3. I was helped on the Spirit's work in Jesus from Sinclair B. Ferguson, *The Holy Spirit*, Contours of Christian Theology (Downers Grove, IL: InterVarsity Press, 1996), 36–56.

4. William L. Lane, *Hebrews 9–13*, Word Biblical Commentary 47B (Dallas: Word, 1991), 240.

5. The translation of *pneumati* as either "spirit" or "Spirit" is debated. The ESV reads: "For Christ also suffered once for sins, the righteous for the unrighteous, that he might bring us to God, being put to death in the flesh but made alive in the spirit." This contrasts two spheres, that of the flesh with that of the spirit. I regard Paul J. Achtemeier's reasoning for adopting "Spirit" as cogent; *1 Peter*, Hermeneia (Minneapolis: Fortress, 1996), 250–51.

6. Paul does the same in 1 Timothy 3:16, when he writes that Jesus was "vindicated by the Spirit."

7. Ben Witherington III, *Conflict and Community in Corinth: A Socio-Rhetorical Commentary on 1 and 2 Corinthians* (Grand Rapids: Eerdmans, 1995), 258.

8. See also Titus 3:4–5: "God . . . saved us, not because of works done by us in righteousness, but according to his own mercy, by the washing of regeneration and renewal of the Holy Spirit."

9. So Constantine R. Campbell, *Paul and Union with Christ: An Exegetical and Theological Study* (Grand Rapids: Zondervan, 2012), 186–87.

10. Peter H. Davids, *The First Epistle of Peter*, New International Commentary on the New Testament (Grand Rapids: Eerdmans, 1990), 168.

Chapter 6: The Holy Spirit's Role in Assurance

1. Graham A. Cole, *He Who Gives Life: The Doctrine of the Holy Spirit*, Foundations of Evangelical Theology (Wheaton, IL: Crossway, 2007), 268–69.

2. "And the Holy Spirit, according to the Holy Scriptures, is neither of the Father alone, nor of the Son alone, but of both; and so intimates to us a mutual love, wherewith the Father and the Son reciprocally love one another" (Augustine, *On the Trinity* 15.17.24, in *A Select Library of the Nicene and Post-Nicene Fathers of the Christian Church*, ed. Philip Schaff [New York: Scribner's, 1917], 3:215).

3. Following Christ's grace and the Father's love, the reference to the Spirit's fellowship suggests "the fellowship we have with one another that the Spirit brings about," Linda L. Belleville, *2 Corinthians*, IVP New Testament Commentary Series (Downers Grove, IL: InterVarsity Press, 1996), 338.

4. "It is the Holy Spirit who stimulates this love." Douglas J. Moo, *The Letters to the Colossians and to Philemon*, Pillar New Testament Commentary (Grand Rapids: Eerdmans, 2008), 92.

5. We are only able to grieve (hurt) the Spirit because he loves us.

6. "The Spirit of grace" is "the Spirit from whom God's grace was

received by the listeners." Peter T. O'Brien, *The Letter to the Hebrews*, Pillar New Testament Commentary (Grand Rapids: Eerdmans, 2010), 379.

7. James D. G. Dunn *Romans 1–8*, Word Biblical Commentary (Dallas: Word, 1988), 253.

8. Dunn *Romans 1–8*, 253.

9. Thomas R. Schreiner, *Romans*, Baker Exegetical Commentary on the New Testament (Grand Rapids: Baker, 1998), 257.

10. See Robert A. Peterson, *Adopted by God* (Phillipsburg, NJ: P&R Publishing, 2001), 59–63.

11. I recommend Sinclair B. Ferguson's edifying, *Children of the Living God* (Edinburgh: Banner of Truth Trust, 1989).

12. See, *Adopted by God*, 145–57.

13. Moo, *The Epistle to the Romans*, 502.

14. C. E. B. Cranfield, *A Critical and Exegetical Commentary on the Epistle to the Romans*, 2 vols., International Critical Commentary (Edinburgh: T&T Clark, 1975), 1:403.

15. Dunn, *Romans 1–8*, 453–54.

16. Thomas R. Schreiner, *Galatians*, Exegetical Commentary on the New Testament (Grand Rapids: Zondervan, 2010), 272, emphasis original.

17. Richard N. Longenecker, *Galatians*, Word Biblical Commentary (Nashville: Nelson, 1990), 174.

18. Longenecker, *Galatians*, 174.

19. Schreiner, *Galatians*, 271, 272.

20. Longenecker, *Galatians*, 174.

21. Robert W. Yarbrough, *1–3 John*, Baker Exegetical Commentary on the New Testament (Grand Rapids: Baker Academic, 2018), 209.

22. Yarbrough, *1–3 John*, 211. Yarbrough quotes Gary M. Burge, *The Letters of John*, NIV Application Commentary (Grand Rapids: Zondervan, 1996), 164.

23. Yarbrough, *1–3 John*, 216.

24. Although they also make sense with what precedes.

25. Yarbrough, *1–3 John*, 246.

26. Yarbrough cogently argues for this rendering. Yarbrough, *1–3 John*, 287n15.

Chapter 7: The Role of Good Works

1. Robert N. Wilkin, "Christians Will Be Judged According to Their Works at the *Rewards* Judgment, but *Not* at the Final Judgment," *The Role of Works at the Final Judgment*, ed. Alan P. Stanley and Stanley N. Gundry, Counterpoints Bible and Theology (Grand Rapids: Zondervan, 2013), 50.

2. Westminster Confession of Faith, ch. 16, "Of Good Works."

3. Leon Morris, *The Gospel according to Matthew*, Pillar New Testament Commentary (Grand Rapids: Eerdmans, 1992), 179.
4. Thomas R. Schreiner, *Galatians,* Exegetical Commentary on the New Testament (Grand Rapids: Zondervan, 2010), 360.
5. John W. Sanderson, *The Fruit of the Spirit* (Phillipsburg, NJ: P&R), 1999.
6. Thomas R. Schreiner, *Galatians*, Zondervan Exegetical Commentary on the New Testament (Grand Rapids: Zondervan, 2010), 348–49.
7. Michael Green, *2 Peter and Jude*, Tyndale New Testament Commentaries (Downers Grove, IL: InterVarsity Press, 2009), 84.
8. Robert W. Yarbrough, *1–3 John*, Baker Exegetical Commentary on the New Testament (Grand Rapids: Baker Academic, 2008), 50.
9. Yarbrough, *1–3 John*, 66.

Chapter 8: The Church and "Defenders" of Assurance

1. Judith M. Gundry Volf, *Paul and Perseverance: Staying In and Falling Away* (Louisville, KY: John Knox, 1990), 53.
2. John Calvin, *Institutes of the Christian Religion* 4.14.6, ed. John T. McNeill, trans. Ford Lewis Battles (Philadelphia: Westminster, 1960), 2:1281; Augustine, *John's Gospel* 80.3 in *Nicene and Post-Nicene Fathers*, ed. Philip Schaff (repr., Grand Rapids: Eerdmans, 1991), 7:344.
3. For more on God's "preaching" the gospel through baptism and the Lord's Supper, see my *Salvation Applied by the Spirit: Union with Christ* (Wheaton, IL: Crossway, 2014), esp. 394–408.
4. Ruth Tucker, *Walking Away from Faith: Unraveling the Mystery of Belief and Unbelief* (Downers Grove, IL: InterVarsity Press, 2002), 26.
5. John Stott, *The Living Church: Convictions of a Lifelong Pastor* (Downers Grove, IL: InterVarsity Press, 2007), 94–95.
6. Stott, *The Living Church*, 87.

SCRIPTURE INDEX

SUBJECT INDEX